MW00444451

History of Armenia

A Captivating Guide to Armenian History, Starting from Ancient Armenia to Its Declaration of Sovereignty from the Soviet Union

© Copyright 2019

All Rights Reserved. No part of this book may be reproduced in any form without permission in writing from the author. Reviewers may quote brief passages in reviews.

Disclaimer: No part of this publication may be reproduced or transmitted in any form or by any means, mechanical or electronic, including photocopying or recording, or by any information storage and retrieval system, or transmitted by email without permission in writing from the publisher.

While all attempts have been made to verify the information provided in this publication, neither the author nor the publisher assumes any responsibility for errors, omissions or contrary interpretations of the subject matter herein.

This book is for entertainment purposes only. The views expressed are those of the author alone, and should not be taken as expert instruction or commands. The reader is responsible for his or her own actions.

Adherence to all applicable laws and regulations, including international, federal, state and local laws governing professional licensing, business practices, advertising and all other aspects of doing business in the US, Canada, UK or any other jurisdiction is the sole responsibility of the purchaser or reader.

Neither the author nor the publisher assumes any responsibility or liability whatsoever on the behalf of the purchaser or reader of these materials. Any perceived slight of any individual or organization is purely unintentional.

Free Bonus from Captivating History (Available for a Limited time)

Hi History Lovers!

Now you have a chance to join our exclusive history list so you can get your first history ebook for free as well as discounts and a potential to get more history books for free! Simply visit the link below to join.

Captivatinghistory.com/ebook

Also, make sure to follow us on Facebook, Twitter and Youtube by searching for Captivating History.

Here is a flag for you, my brother,

that I have sewn by hand

over the sleepless nights

and bathed in my tears.

- Armenian National Anthem

Contents

Introduction

Humanity may have been born in the mountains of Armenia. Biblical accounts tell that it survived there, that after a terrible flood wiped out the human race, a group of people made a fresh start on the flanks of Mount Ararat. And survival has been the theme of this ancient nation's history, a story that is nothing short of epic and inspiring.

The tale of Armenia has its beginnings as a glorious ancient kingdom, one that commanded the respect of nations as mighty as Egypt and Babylonia. As its history takes a turn for the darker, each chapter reads like a roll call of the most famous of figures: Antony and Cleopatra, Alexander the Great, Genghis Khan, Frederick Barbarossa. Armenia saw ancient Rome rise to power; it knew Egyptian pharaohs, the Golden Horde, the Soviet Union, and saw the first invasion of the first Muslim army. For a long and ugly part of its history, Armenia struggled under the yokes of one empire after another: the Roman, Parthian, Persian, Byzantine, Timurid, Mongolian, and Ottoman Empires, to name just a few.

Yet through it all, Armenia, time and time again, emerged as a nation with a powerful identity, one that caused much grief over the years, but one that still remains a pillar of strength to its people in good times and in bad. There is much sorrow held within these pages; much oppression, much persecution, and even the most terrible evil of them all—genocide. The reading is made easy by one single gleaming light, a golden thread running through every word and chapter, and that light is the Armenian people themselves.

Their story is tragic, but their survival is incredible. And that is what makes their tale so inspiring.

Chapter 1 – The Home of Eden

And a river went out of Eden to water the garden; and from thence it was parted, and became into four heads. The name of the first *is* Pison: that *is* it which compasseth the whole land of Havilah, where *there* *is* gold; And the gold of that land *is* good: there *is* bdellium and the onyx stone. And the name of the second river *is* Gihon: the same *is* it that compasseth the whole land of Ethiopia. And the name of the third river *is* Hiddekel: that *is* it which goeth toward the east of Assyria. And the fourth river *is* Euphrates.

- Genesis 2:10-14

For millennia, Christian scholars have searched for the Garden of Eden, the biblical home of the birth of mankind. These scholars speculate that one of the most likely locations for the home of Eden is in the heart of one of the most ancient countries in the world: Armenia. With four rivers flowing through its abundant landscape—including those still known today as the Tigris and Euphrates—Armenia is one of the oldest homes of the human race. To paraphrase the British admiral John Byron, according to biblical beliefs, Adam was created from the dust of Armenia.

In fact, with its modern-day capital Yerevan nestled on the flanks of Mount Ararat, Armenia may be the biblical location not only of the birth of humankind but also one of rebirth: it was on Mount Ararat that Noah's ark was beached after the flood, according to scriptures.

Regardless of where that biblical garden may be located, it is certain that Armenia has been home to humanity for many, many thousands of years.

* * * *

5,500 years ago—around 3500 BCE—a lonely figure strode across the soaring landscapes of his ancient paradise. Surrounded by the towering walls of mountain peaks, the man paused on the rocky hilltop, gazing at the majesty of the surrounding countryside. Rivers and lakes were splashes of blue in the valleys below; the icy wind combed the waving grass of the harsh mountainside where the man stood. Around him, a flock of sheep picked at the grass, seeking out sustenance where they could in this beautiful, bleak landscape.

Their shepherd had a mane of scarlet hair that tossed in the cold breeze. It was a splash of fire among the more neutral colors of the surroundings, and it crowned a figure that looked different from the people of today, one that was shorter and more powerfully built. The young man's eyes were piercing as he gazed out across the mountainous region where he had made his home. He shifted his weight, feeling his feet safely encased inside the leather shoes that covered them. Other peoples of the age wore sandals, but in the chill of the mountains, closed shoes were essential.

The red-haired man paused only for a moment before heading off again, summoning his sheep and moving purposefully across the flank of the mountain. And little did he know that his simple leather shoe—made from cowhide and carefully sewn into shape—would be discovered 5,500 years later and make history as the oldest shoe ever discovered.

Known as the Areni-1 shoe, this ancient piece of footwear, which is older than Stonehenge, was found in a cave complex near the modern-day village of Areni, Armenia. It was a testimony to the Chalcolithic period, a transitional period between the Stone Age and the Bronze Age, and the people that have lived in this ancient country for so many years. Perfectly preserved in layers of droppings from the sheep that ancient Armenians kept, it was even stuffed with grass, possibly in an attempt to keep its shape. The Chalcolithic period featured the first use of metal, giving it the colloquial name of the Copper Age—a somewhat poetic name, considering that DNA found in the same caves as the shoe indicated that at least one of the cave's ancient inhabitants had red hair and blue eyes.

Little is known of these ancient Armenians, and even less is known of the other cultures around that period, but we do know that humans have been living there for a very long time. The Areni-1 cave complex gave rise to numerous important discoveries from even before the time of our redheaded shepherd. Burial sites that were from as many as 6,000 years ago have been discovered there since the excavation began by an Irish-Armenian team in 2007; for example, a skull from a preteen, found in a clay pot, yielded a sample of amazingly well-preserved brain tissue from the Stone Age. There was even a winepress in those caves, making it the oldest winery ever discovered. In fact, the shoes we imagined on the feet of our shepherd may actually have been designed for trampling grapes to release their juice and turn it into an ancient alcoholic drink that we still enjoy today.

The Shulaveri-Shomu culture was one of the earliest known cultures to live in Armenia; they were around a little before our well-shod redhead, living there around 4000 BCE. These were followed by the Bronze Age Kura-Araxes culture, named after one of the rivers where they made their home, the Araxes (whose name means "fast-flowing" or "dashing," the same as the name Gihon, mentioned in the biblical account of the Garden of Eden's location). Finally, the Trialeti-Vanadzor culture, existing around 1600 BCE, made their homes in Armenia and its surroundings, including modern-day Turkey and Georgia.

One of the very first ancient Armenians whom we know by name is a folk hero from about 2500 BCE—about a thousand years after the lifetime of the wearer of that ancient shoe. His story is so old and so steeped in tradition that his very existence is questionable. However, where archaeology has failed to discover the exact origins of the Armenian people, their traditions have, for centuries, traced back to a single hero: Hayk Nahapet.

* * * *

"Nahapet" means "patriarch" in Armenian, and Hayk is looked upon as the progenitor of all the Armenian people. According to tradition, he originally served Nimrod, a hunter, warrior, king, and the founder of Babylonia. A subject of the ancient empire of Babylon, Hayk grew tired of its new king, Bel, and emigrated to the shadow of Mount Ararat, where the bones of Noah's ark still rested on the mountaintop.

Founding a village that he named after himself, Hayk tried to settle down with his family, despite Bel's pleas for him to return. When Hayk continued to refuse to go back to Babylon, the petulant king turned angry. He marched on Hayk's village with a vast army, determined to raze Haykashen to the ground.

But Hayk would not be so easily cowed. He had learned in the shadow of Nimrod, a heroic warrior who had built the empire that Bel was abusing. He armed himself with a bow and gathered his army on the shores of Lake Van, and there, where the great lake lay like a pool of liquid glass among the sentinel figures of the mountains, the Battle of the Giants took place.

When the Babylonians came pouring down the mountainside, Hayk was quick to spot Bel's hated visage among the churning mass of the vanguard. Stringing an arrow, he raised his bow, drawing it with his powerful arms. His glittering eyes focused on the chest of his great enemy, and even though the world rang with the battle cries of Babylonian and Haykashen citizens, Hayk heard nothing but the soft creak of his bow. He breathed out and fired the arrow. It lanced through the air, an impossibly long shot. It couldn't possibly make it. Hayk's tiny army was doomed in the face of the might of Babylonia.

Except it wasn't. True and fierce, the arrow arced through the air and plunged deep into Bel's heart. He collapsed, and his army was thrown into disarray. Hayk and his men rushed forward, and the defeat of the Babylonians was complete.

* * * *

The traditional date of the legendary Battle of Giants is August 11th, 2492 BCE. How much of the story is true is unknown; however, to this day, the Armenian word for an Armenian person is *hay*, and for Armenia, *Hayk'*.

By 1446 BCE, the nation founded on Hayk's single arrow had become known as Hayastan, or the Hayasa-Azzi kingdom. It had risen in prominence to become one of the greatest of ancient powers, revered even by the Egyptian pharaoh of the time. Thutmose III was arguably the most powerful pharaoh of ancient Egypt, as he controlled the largest empire of any pharaoh, stretching all the way from Syria to Nubia after seventeen campaigns were launched to expand his territory. But Hayastan never fell to Thutmose's blade. He called it Ermenen, one of the earliest references to Armenia that resembles its modern English name, and wrote at length about its beauty. "Heaven rests upon its four pillars," he said.

By 1200 BCE, as the Bronze Age began to reach its end, the Hayasa-Azzi kingdom had faded from the pages of history. The former unity of the kingdom was gone, replaced by different tribes scattered across the face of Armenia, but the people still understood that there was power in standing together, even though their kingdom had fallen. A confederation of tribes was established in the Armenian highlands around that same lake where Hayk had made his fateful stand. This confederation was named "Nairi" ("Land of Rivers") by its greatest enemies, the neighboring and powerful Assyrians. Yet the Assyrians were unable to defeat the Nairi. Absorbing the peoples of the Hayasa-Azzi kingdom, the Nairi was a formidable force, strong enough to withstand the onslaught of both the Assyrians and the Hittites.

For the next four hundred years, the Nairi would be the glowing height of Armenian power. But the power to follow, a kingdom founded around the mountain where Noah's ark had landed, would prove to be even greater still.

Chapter 2 – The Rise and Fall of Urartu

Considering that the Kingdom of Urartu was only really discovered by archaeologists in the 19th century CE, after having disappeared from history for almost a thousand years, it is unsurprising that the name might sound unfamiliar to the contemporary reader. Urartu was an Assyrian name for the great kingdom that was born from the womb of the Nairi, but its Hebrew name would be familiar to the modern ear: Ararat, the same as the biblical mountain at whose feet the kingdom grew up.

Those same Assyrians who named Urartu were the very threat that forced the Nairi to become more than just a confederation of tribes and petty little kingdoms. The Assyrian Empire—known as the first true empire in history—was one of the most formidable forces in the world at that point. Its last incarnation, the Neo-Assyrian Empire, was also its strongest; starting from 911 BCE, it proved to be almost impossible to defeat. Powers as great as Egypt and Jerusalem fell before its charging hordes of soldiers and chariots, and there was nothing that could stand against it.

Compared with the might of Jerusalem that had fallen almost entirely in the face of the Assyrians, the Nairi were nobodies. There was no way that their little confederation could hope to stand against Assyria—or at least, so it looked on paper. But there was a powerful leader determined to rise up against the marauding invaders, a man who was ready to do whatever it took to defend his people and his kingdom. And that man would become King Arame, the first king of Urartu.

Arame was a leader so powerful that he eventually became legendary. Armenian tradition likely bases one of its greatest heroes—Ara the Beautiful—on this first great king. Ara the Beautiful was a warrior so noble and handsome that he attracted the attentions of Semiramis, a sorceress. When Ara scorned her, Semiramis declared war on his kingdom, ordering her soldiers to capture Ara alive. Somehow, Ara was killed, and the distraught Semiramis raised him from the dead, causing the end of the war with his kingdom.

While it is unlikely that necromancy was part of Arame's true story, he was certainly a very capable leader since he managed to stand against the Assyrian king, Shalmaneser III. Forging the diverse group of tribes into a single united front ready to stand against the Assyrians, Arame was made the first king of the Nairi in 858 BCE. Under his leadership, the Nairi put up a spirited defense. Shalmaneser did succeed in capturing the capital, but their lands were not wholly defeated, and its rulers kept it from the clutches of Assyria for centuries to come.

Arame laid the foundation for a kingdom that would grow to become one of the greatest powers in the ancient Middle East. By the end of his rule, Armenia was no longer simply a confederation called the Nairi—it was a kingdom, the Kingdom of Urartu. He was succeeded by Sarduri I, whose ancestry is disputed; he may have been Arame's son, but some sources call him the son of Lutipri, therefore making him a usurper. Regardless of the legitimacy of Sarduri's claim to the throne, he followed in Arame's footsteps as a strong leader. Having lost the former capital of the kingdom to the Assyrians, Sarduri continued to work on unifying his people. He built a new capital in

830 BCE, laying its foundations on a limestone promontory on the eastern shore of Lake Van—the very place where the legendary Hayk had taken his stand against the enemy hordes.

The new city, named Tushpa, would later be known as Van. For now, however, its stone citadel was a stronghold that Sarduri hoped would be able to withstand the invading Assyrians. His hopes would come true; while Shalmaneser continued his attempts to invade Urartu, Sarduri's defenses were, for the most part, successful. Urartu was starting to find its way onto the map as the strange little kingdom that the Assyrians just could not beat.

Sarduri's successor, Ishpuini, took the throne after Sarduri's death in 828 BCE. Tushpa was just two years old at that point, but already, Urartu was feeling the effects of increased security throughout the land. In fact, Ishpuini was the first Urartian king who could turn his attention from defense to offense. He was, of course, not foolish enough to attack the Assyrians. Instead, he set his sights on an easier target: the city of Musasir. It is uncertain where exactly Musasir was located—an archaeological site near Lake Urmia in Iran is one of the potential locations—but the city and its surroundings bordered on Urartu, and Ishpuini wanted them. He annexed the city and then turned his attention to religion and culture instead of war. The Urartians had a unique polytheistic religion, and Ishpuini seemed to be a devoted follower. He made Musasir the religious center of Urartu and made regular pilgrimages there, introducing his people to the cult of Haldi, who was a warrior god who could have possibly been the Urartian god of the sun as well. Ishpuini was also the first Urartian king to keep his records in his native language.

King Menua, who co-ruled with Ishpuini, helped to expand the borders of the growing kingdom even farther. By the time he became the sole ruler in approximately 810 BCE, the kingdom was no longer known by its own name as the kingdom of the Nairi. Instead, it was given a new moniker: *Bianili*, or "from Biani," the Urartian name for the region around Lake Van.

The Assyrians were going through a period of stagnation themselves, and so, the Urartians were able to keep their focus on increasing their power rather than defending it. This led to a period of prosperity for the everyday people of Urartu, and they developed a fascinating and complicated culture. Like their ancestors from prehistoric times, the Urartians were winemakers and shepherds, but they were perhaps most gifted in raising horses. The rocky highlands held rich grazing for the animals that were strong and tough enough to climb the mountainsides to get to it; this led to the breeding of hardy horses that, when brought down from the mountains, had a greater lung capacity than their lowland cousins. They could outrun any Assyrian horse harnessed to a chariot, leading to a growing trade of horses between Urartu and Assyria in times of peace. The Urartians were also some of the earliest horsemen, riding astride their swift animals rather than riding only in chariots.

Art was another favorite occupation for the Urartians. They built extravagant temples, commonly using the limestone that was so profuse in the region, and decorated them with stone carvings and inscriptions, as well as painting on the plastered walls. Vibrant blues and reds were their favorite colors, and the Urartians depicted scenes from their lives and faith. They were also gifted metalworkers; everything from statues to hinges could be made out of bronze, and as the Iron Age dawned across civilization, Urartians soon learned these skills, too.

Under the rule of Argishti I in the 8th century BCE, Urartu reached the height of its power. Its borders encompassed parts of modern-day Armenia, Turkey, Georgia, and Iran, and it was a formidable power that rose up in a time when Assyria was crushing everything in its path. Yet even though it had once made peace with its oldest enemy, Urartu would fall victim to an Assyrian invasion. And this time, there would be no Arame to save it.

* * * *

King Rusa I of Urartu had been brought to the very brink of despair.

Tiglath-Pileser III, the same biblical Assyrian king who had terrorized the lands of Israel and Judah, had spent the early years of Rusa I's reign—in the late 8th century BCE—decimating Urartu. The Assyrian king had seized many of Urartu's lands and laid waste to both their cities and their economy before leaving the crippled kingdom a mere shadow of the great power it had been under Argishti I. And while Tiglath-Pileser III had died in 727 BCE, the period of rest that Urartu had experienced after his death turned out not to be a path to new prosperity but simply a breather. Sargon II ascended the throne in 722 BCE, and in 715 BCE, he set his sights on a nation that had been a thorn in the side of Assyria since its inception: Urartu.

The Urartu-Assyrian War had been raging for two long, hard, devastating years, having started in 714 BCE. Like all the Urartian kings before him, Rusa I had not relied on generals to lead his men into battle. Instead, he had been at the forefront of every fight, swinging his own sword into the butchering masses of the invaders, and he had personally witnessed one defeat after the other. Urartu's depleted resources were no match for Assyria at the height of its power, and Sargon II was sowing destruction everywhere he went.

To make matters even worse, the Cimmerians—nomads from the Caucasus—chose the year 714 BCE, the height of the war with Assyria, to attempt to invade Urartu. Rusa did his best to fight two wars at once, but it was clear that Urartu was being crushed between the scissor blades of two enemies, and it did not help that this was happening at the tail end of decades of oppression.

Now, Rusa was facing not only the threat of his enemies but also utter humiliation and the loss of a city that was at the very heart of the Urartian faith and people. The Battle of Mount Waush had been a rare victory for Rusa, and when he had routed Sargon and put his troops to flight, the king had begun to hope that perhaps the tide was turning. Maybe Urartu was going to make it out of this after all. But Sargon's pride had been deeply wounded by the way he had been forced to turn tail and run, and he was bent on getting his revenge on

Rusa. There was no city that meant more to Rusa and his people than Musasir, and so, Sargon set the holy city of Urartu alight.

The news of Musasir's burning would have been to Rusa what it would have been for a Muslim to hear of the sacking of Mecca. It was a devastating blow, and one that was too much for a king who had already suffered desperately during his reign. Most of his years as king had been occupied in hopeless warfare, and Rusa knew he was watching his kingdom slide away into oblivion and that he was helpless to stop it. Faced with the despair of his people as their beloved city was torched to ashes, Rusa could not see any way out. So, he took his own weapon and killed himself.

With their king dead, the Urartians had little option but to negotiate a surrender with the Assyrians. They were forced to pay tribute to Assyria, which was a crippling amount considering the toll that years of warfare had taken on their failing economy.

Nevertheless, refusing to give up, Rusa's son, Argishti II, followed in the footsteps of his powerful namesake by attempting to restore Urartu to some semblance of the greatness it had enjoyed during the 9th century. As Urartu limped into the 7th century BCE, Argishti managed to nurse the economy back to health, despite the tribute owed to Assyria, and Urartian culture managed to flourish in the face of adversity for another century. It was only around 612 BCE, when the Medes and the Scythians joined forces to conquer Assyria, that Urartu finally fell. The Medes invaded it and took its capital, by then known as Van, in 590 BCE.

Urartu was gone, but its people lived on, oppressed though they were by the Medes and the Scythians. Sadly for them, this was only their first taste of oppression. The centuries that followed would see a string of conquerors coming for the natural resources so richly present in Urartu, which would soon become known by a different name, a name that endures to this day: Armenia.

Chapter 3 – A Conquered Armenia

Compared with other ancient powers, little is known about the race that captured Urartu in 585 BCE. The Medes were a mysterious group whose origins are shrouded in mystery. They had been living in the land of Media—part of modern-day Iran—for centuries, but they had been little more than a scattered group of tribes pretending to be a kingdom until Cyaxares became their first truly ambitious king and forged an empire out of them in 625 BCE. Within a few years, Cyaxares had captured the city of Nineveh, thereby conquering the Assyrians and making Media one of the most important powers of the ancient Middle East. By comparison, the weakened Urartu had been easy pickings.

Yet the glory day of the Medes would not last forever. No empire ever did, and Media would only continue unconquered for around 75 years before it, too, would meet its match in the form of another one of the greatest powers in antiquity: the first Persian Empire, also known as the Achaemenid Empire.

It is seldom that a conquering ruler, a man who built a vast empire and one who would go down in history with the epithet "the great," a man of war and incredible power, is remembered as being a merciful and benevolent king. Cyrus the Great was one of those men.

Legend has it that Cyrus was the crown prince of Media, but a prophetic dream caused his father, King Astyages, to throw him out into the wilderness when he was a baby. Cyrus was raised by lowly herders and returned to conquer the kingdom that was rightfully his, despite his humble upbringing. It is more likely that he was the son of a minor king in Astyages' realm and became the king of Persis in the early 6th century BCE. Either way, he might have borne the title of king, but he was a nobody—just another of Astyages' servants. That was the case until 550 BCE. Gathering a puny army, Cyrus set his sights on Ecbatana, the capital of Media and the seat of Astyages. Potentially with help from the Median commander—who was also sick of Astyages' rule—Cyrus conquered his overlord and became the most powerful man on the Iranian Plateau. He crowned himself king of Persia and was determined to build a far greater realm than Media had ever been.

And build a mighty realm he did. Cyrus would go on to defeat even the might of Babylon, then one of the greatest powers of the known world, without spilling a drop of blood. The people had heard of his benevolence and goodness to those he ruled over, and they threw the gates wide before him. Indeed, having overthrown the brutal oppressors who formerly ruled over Babylon, Cyrus was the one who set free the captive Jews, and in doing so, he probably saved the Jewish faith (and the following Christian one) from obscurity. He is also credited with composing the Cyrus Cylinder, the first known bill of human rights, which stipulated that his subjects be allowed to live peacefully and practice their own culture and religion under his rule.

Cyrus the Great did succeed in founding a great empire, known as the Achaemenid Empire. And given that he had annexed all of the Median lands, Urartu—by then becoming known as Armenia—fell under Cyrus' rule. The people that were left after war and economic failure had crippled the kingdom were briefly permitted to live in some form of peace. But by 530 BCE, Cyrus was dead, most likely falling in a fight with rebellious nomads on the borders of his kingdom. And the Achaemenid kings that followed would prove to be far less kind—and far more typical of powerful kings—than their predecessor.

Soon, the Armenians, which were by then a race impoverished by the destruction of war, found themselves being deeply oppressed by the people who now ruled them. The Achaemenids began to tax Armenia heavily, and they wanted something that Armenia had only the very best of: horses. Fast, tough, and strong, Armenian horses were coveted for the constant warfare of an expanding empire, and the Achaemenids wanted lots and lots of them. In fact, Armenia had to pay an annual tax of 20,000 strong colts to the Achaemenid Persians. For a country whose economy was based on the production of young horses, this was a devastating blow.

The once-vibrant culture that had flourished during the glory days of Urartu now found itself crushed under the suffocating weight of necessity. The people who had been so dedicated to art and metalwork were now simply trying to make ends meet. They lived in small villages on the mountainsides in underground dwellings, no longer building strong stone homes or bustling cities. In fact, they were reduced to becoming semi-nomadic; depending entirely on flocks of sheep and herds of cattle or horses that the Armenians kept, they were forced to follow the grazing patterns, moving from summer to winter pastures. Even the stately vineyards that had once fueled the oldest winery in existence had disappeared. Instead, fields of barley had to be planted to be eaten as a staple. What little was left over was brewed into simple beer instead of the ancient wines that the people had once enjoyed.

In strong contrast to their suffering subjects, the government officials of Armenia (now a satrapy, or province, of the Achaemenid Empire) lived in comfort, pomp, and splendor. They had large houses with plenty of room to store all of the delicacies that the Armenians had been able to indulge in before the fall of Urartu, which included wine, beef, and raisins. And with tens of thousands of horses being shipped off so that Armenia's conquerors could go off and subjugate other nations just like them, there was no way that the common Armenian could find a way back to financial stability.

To rub salt in the wound, the shining culture of Armenia was shattered to its very core; even its religion was changed. While there is little evidence to suggest forced conversion, somehow during the two hundred years of the Achaemenid occupation of Armenia, the ancient faith of the Armenians was stripped away. In its place, the Armenians began to practice the same religion as the rest of the empire: Zoroastrianism.

One of the oldest monotheistic religions in the world, the origins of Zoroastrianism are obscure. Some say that it emerged around 1500 BCE; others claim that it found its roots around the time of Cyrus the Great. Either way, its first practitioner was a former polytheistic prophet by the name of Zoroaster. He told his followers about a vision he had received of a single ruling god, an idea that was utterly alien in a region that was mostly worshiping gods of the sun and sea. His ideas spread as far as the Achaemenids conquered, and it became the major religion of most of the Middle East and Asia until it was supplanted by Islam after the Muslim conquest of Persia around 651 CE.

To the Armenians, Zoroastrianism was a completely foreign concept, an idea far removed from the gods that their grandparents had worshiped. Yet it wormed its way into their hearts and homes, stripping away the relics of what they had once believed, the code by which their lives had once been lived. Their old faith was thrown to the wayside, and eventually, the majority of Armenia believed as their conquerors did.

The conditions chafed at the bruised Armenian psyche: the suffering, the struggle, and the knowledge that the taxes that hurt them were equally hurting other countries. For almost two hundred years,

Armenia continued to suffer, but rebellion was brewing in the fertile ground of discontent.

Ever since it fell into the hands of the Achaemenids, the Satrapy of Armenia was ruled over by a satrap, or governor. In the 4th century BCE, one of these satraps would rise up in defense of his people.

Potentially Armenian by blood, in contrast with most satraps who were of Achaemenid royalty, Orontes I probably earned his way to his title as satrap of Armenia by proving himself in battle, fighting on the behalf of King Artaxerxes II against rebels in Cyprus. When Artaxerxes tried to order Orontes to move to a different satrapy, however, Orontes rebelled against him.

Orontes was not the only satrap who wanted change. Datames, satrap of Cappadocia, and Ariobarzanes, satrap of Phrygia, had also been fighting for change since 372 BCE in what is now called the Great Satraps' Revolt. Soon finding the support of the Egyptian pharaoh, Nectanebo I (whose successors would also aid in the fight, as Egypt was often an enemy of the Achaemenid Empire), the disgruntled satraps started to push back against their oppressive superiors. Orontes joined the fight in 362 BCE, ten years after Datames had begun the revolt, and at first, things looked promising for the people who trusted in him as being a savior. But their trust was deeply misplaced. Thanks to Egyptian help, the satraps succeeded militarily in many ways against the Achaemenids. The might of the Persian Empire was unable to crush the rebellion on the battlefield. Instead, it would be lost to the slow cancer of treachery, eating its way through the very heart of the revolt.

Ariobarzanes was the first to fall. Even though he had been supported by the powerful king of Sparta for three years, he failed to gain the support of his own son, Mithridates, who betrayed him to Artaxerxes II. The king had Ariobarzanes crucified and killed in 363 BCE. The following year, Datames was likewise betrayed, this time by his son-in-law.

The final blow to end the revolt came shortly thereafter. Nobody betrayed Orontes; instead, the Armenian satrap betrayed his own people. He turned against the revolt that he had once supported, and the Great Satraps' Revolt ended in ignominy and defeat. Orontes, however, was richly rewarded for ending the revolt; he was given many of the lands that had formerly belonged to Datames, his former comrade, and was allowed to keep his title as satrap of Armenia. Orontes' descendants would hold on to the title, too, making him the founder of the Orontid dynasty of Armenian satraps and, later, kings.

Despite the failure of the revolt, it would not be long before Armenia was freed from the fist of the Achaemenids. But, at least for a brief time, this freedom would catapult them out of the frying pan and into the fire. The Achaemenids were about to be defeated—not by their own unhappy people but by a far greater power. A young but nonetheless battle-hardened warlord, charging from the lands of the east, against whose fearsome armies not even the Achaemenid Empire could hope to stand a chance.

* * * *

Alexander was recovering from an illness, was vastly outnumbered, and had lived fewer years than the experienced commanders of the Achaemenid armies had been fighting battles. But he still believed that Persia would soon be his.

Only 23 years old, Alexander had been ruling over Macedonia for three years since the assassination of his father, Philip II. To honor his dead father's memory, Alexander was determined to finish what Philip had started: the conquest of Persia. Even though this quest may have seemed foolhardy for a mere youth with little experience to back him, Alexander believed that the gods were with him. Legend told how he had solved the unsolvable by untying the Gordian Knot (or, more accurately, sliced it in half) and how thunderstorms had been a good omen before the battle. But it was more than just luck that would play into Alexander's impending success: it was military brilliance.

Persian King Darius III had not yet fully tasted the young Macedonian's true skill. With an army 100,000 strong, Darius believed that not only could he put Alexander's troops to flight, but he could also cut off their retreat and butcher the lot of them, putting a stop to Macedonian aspirations once and for all. He could not have been more wrong.

There were about 40,000 Armenians in Darius' army the day that he met with Alexander on the coastal plains near Issus. Alexander, on the other hand, commanded about 30,000 men, his troops decimated by malaria and months of fighting. Yet the fiery young king, mounted on his trusted old black charger Bucephalus, inspired a blazing hope in his men and commanded them adeptly. Using the harsh terrain to his advantage, Alexander fought in the foremost ranks of his soldiers, tricking the Persians' experienced mercenaries into going toward perceived gaps in his offense that put them right where he wanted him. Within a few hours, the Achaemenid Empire had been put to flight. Darius III was captured, and the Achaemenid Empire was no more.

As for the Armenians, who fought for an empire that had been taxing them so harshly for so many years, many of their numbers died as they had lived: cut down, bruised, and crushed on behalf of the Achaemenid Empire.

Chapter 4 – An Empire in its Own Right

Illustration I: The Armenian Empire at its apogee under Tigranes the Great, also known as Tigran

The life of Alexander the Great was a shooting star, a blazing comet that shone as bright as it was brief. Conquering Persia was just the start of his military success. The Battle of Issus made the way clear for him to march into the heart of Persia, and from there, he took Egypt in 331 BCE, followed by parts of Iran, India, and Babylon (modern-day Iraq). Nothing and no one could stand against him. He was the king of the known world, and he had expanded the borders of his tiny realm farther than even his ambitious father could have imagined.

In fact, Alexander's impact may have been even greater if a twist of fate had not cut short the illustrious life of this young emperor. He had his sights set on defeating Carthage and even Rome. If he had conquered the Roman Empire, the face of history might have looked very different. However, Rome would rule for over a thousand more years, thanks to a bout of malaria that claimed Alexander's life in 323 BCE. He was only 32.

While Alexander had expanded the borders of his kingdom, he had not given much thought to what would happen to it after he died, and immediately, the vast empire was in desperate peril. Alexander's wife, Roxana, was pregnant, and in his jealous rage, Alexander had killed every other male with any claim to the throne. While a regent, Perdiccas, was appointed, he decided to divide up Alexander's empire among a bunch of satraps. This was a fatal mistake. The satraps soon fell to fighting, trying to gain independence for their satrapies or even to seize the Macedonian crown for themselves. As quickly as Alexander's giant empire had been won, it melted just as quickly into chaos.

* * * *

For Armenia, the entire rule of Alexander had been a time of uncertainty. Things in the Achaemenid Empire had been difficult, but at least they had been familiar. Besides that, Armenia was starting to prove itself as one of the Achaemenid Empire's most important satrapies. Darius III, the man who had been ruling over the empire at the time of its fall, had been a satrap of Armenia himself before becoming king. Maybe things were beginning to look up.

Maybe they would be worse under Alexander.

Alexander, however, had far bigger fish to fry than Armenia. It appears as though he might not have ever officially occupied it; he even allowed Orontes II, the satrap at the time, to keep his title. When Alexander's empire crumbled, Orontes saw his chance. Unlike his namesake—and likely his ancestor—who had betrayed his own people in the Great Satraps' Revolt, Orontes II wanted to build a better Armenia. For the first time in centuries, Armenia had the opportunity to be free.

This time, Orontes was successful. With the Macedonians fighting over the scraps, he was able to establish Armenia as an independent kingdom, ushering in the Orontid dynasty. His descendants would no more be satraps; instead, they were kings of a country all its own.

For over a hundred years, the Orontids ruled over an independent Armenia, slowly putting back together a country ravished by centuries of occupation. They were able to restore Armenia to something of its former glory, with new cities springing up everywhere. No longer did all the Armenians have to live in underground dwellings with their flocks and herds.

The Orontid dynasty, however, would be relatively short-lived. A beast had risen from the ashes of Alexander's empire—and that beast was hungry.

* * * *

Alexander's death fragmented his empire, and one of the bigger chunks would someday become a Hellenistic empire itself, forged by a man named Seleucus.

Placed in charge of Babylon under Perdiccas' regency, Seleucus, a Greek, was one of the satraps who wanted more. He won independence for his country, naming it the Seleucid Kingdom. It did not take long for the kingdom to become an empire, encompassing parts of Parthia, Greece, and India. And despite a crippling civil war just a generation ago, which saw the Seleucid Empire lose many of its lands, by the late 2nd century BCE, a new ruler had risen up. One who was determined not only to restore the empire to its former glory but to expand it even further.

Antiochus III the Great was more than just a king in the eyes of his subjects. He was a deity. Having established a cult around himself and his consort, he made himself vitally important to the people, gaining their wholehearted support for his campaigns. He was able to win back many of the eastern lands that had been lost during the civil war between his father and uncle, as well as conquering Lebanon and Palestine. It didn't take long before he set his sights on gaining even more lands—and Armenia was among them.

In 200 BCE, Orontes IV was overthrown by the Seleucid Empire, making him the last of the Orontid kings. Much of Armenia was brought under Seleucid control, at least for a brief time, as Antiochus plowed over his latest conquest and headed toward Rome. It would have been wiser to leave the mighty Roman Empire alone, though. The Romans defeated him in battle in 190 BCE and reduced his empire to only a handful of countries, effectively ending the Seleucid Empire when Antiochus was killed in 187 BCE, although it did manage to hang on, albeit weakly, until 63 BCE.

During the brief Seleucid occupation, Armenia had been divided into two separate satraps: Lesser Armenia and Greater Armenia. It was ruled over by a father and son named Zariadres and Artaxias, both Seleucid satraps that Antiochus had appointed. When Artaxias heard of Antiochus' defeat by the Romans, he knew that the Seleucid Empire had sung its swansong. It would soon crumble into nothing, and then it would be every man for himself. There was danger in the situation but also opportunity.

It was an opportunity that Artaxias would seize with both hands. Setting himself up as the king of Greater Armenia, Artaxias I started to move to secure power for his country. Largely supported by the people, who had enjoyed their freedom under the Orontids (to whom Artaxias and Zariadres may have been related), Artaxias expanded Greater Armenia's borders and established it as a country in its own right once more. He was able to unify its diverse and scattered peoples and became one of the most famed governors of Armenia since its ancient beginnings. Immortalized in legend and song, Artaxias took advantage of the fact that trade routes between Rome and India ran through the country. Armenia flourished, and by 176 BCE, Artaxias was able to build a whole new city for his capital. Known as Artaxata, it may have been designed by the legendary Carthaginian general, Hannibal Barca.

Artaxias I became the founder of one of Armenia's most glorious dynasties: the Artaxiad dynasty. For almost a hundred years, one Artaxiad king after the other governed the country well enough that it was able to stand its ground in an era of relentless expansion and conquest. Artaxias had made Armenia an ally of Rome, and the Romans were all too happy to have Armenia as a buffer between their empire and their great enemies, the Parthians. But even Artaxias was nothing compared to the greatest of the Artaxiad kings. In 95 BCE, this great warrior ruler would rise to the throne. And despite unpromising beginnings, Tigranes II would prove to be the mightiest king of them all.

* * * *

Tigranes had been a prisoner for more than half of his life.

He had been only twenty years old when the Parthians, an old enemy of both Rome and Armenia, had finally gained the upper hand in their repeated attempts to invade Armenia. Mithridates II, the king of Parthia, had seized some parts of the country, and the current king of Armenia—Artavasdes I—was forced to negotiate peace or risk losing his entire kingdom. Artavasdes and the Parthians came to an accord at last in 120 BCE, but it was one that would be devastating for Artavasdes. He was forced to give up the parts of Armenia that Mithridates had annexed, and he was also forced to give up his relative, Tigranes. Sources differ on whether Tigranes was his son, brother, or nephew, but either way, the young man was a free Armenian, an heir to the throne, and shared a blood bond with Artavasdes. But the king had no choice. He had to send Tigranes to Parthia to become their hostage.

For the next 25 years, Tigranes would be trapped in a Parthian fortress. It is likely that he lived in a fair amount of luxury during that time and that his needs were well provided for, but one can only imagine how his heart longed for the wide skies, soaring mountains, and wild highlands of his youth. Tigranes had walked the mountainsides of Armenia not only as a free citizen but also as its future king. Now he was nothing but a pawn in the Parthians' game, an incentive for the Armenian king to keep the peace with Parthia or risk the death of the crown prince.

But Tigranes used that quarter-century in captivity wisely. He gained the Parthians' trust and learned their ways, and when the king of Armenia, Tigranes I, died in 95 BCE, Parthia decided that having a tame little king on the Armenian throne would do nothing but advance their own interests. Mithridates made the decision: Tigranes would be going home, as long as he yielded even more of Armenia's lands to the Parthians.

Tigranes, appearing as meek as a lamb, readily agreed. He ceded seventy valleys to the Parthians and made his way back to the land that he loved, finally taking the throne that was rightfully his. He must have been aware that the Parthians believed he would do whatever they asked and remain an easily manipulated ally.

They could not have been more wrong.

Knowing that Armenia needed help from a strong ally, Tigranes was quick to find a suitable princess to marry and thus gain the favor of her powerful father. That princess was Cleopatra the Elder, a princess of Pontus, which was a small but powerful nation on the banks of the Black Sea in modern-day Turkey. Less than a year into his reign, the new king began to expand his realm. His first aim was to annex Lesser Armenia, thereby unifying the two countries once again; he succeeded in this by 94 BCE.

In 91 BCE, Mithridates II—the same king that had held Tigranes captive for 25 years—died. Parthia was left in utter chaos, and Tigranes saw his chance to break free at last from the Parthian shackles and build the empire of which he had been dreaming all those long and weary years in captivity. He attacked the Parthians on the eastern border, wiping them out of the seventy valleys and regaining them for Armenia. This left no doubt in the Parthians' minds that the young man they had held captive for so many years was not going to kowtow to them any longer. Tigranes was no client king: he was a conqueror, and he was going to show the world what he could do.

Starting his campaign in 88 BCE, Tigranes did exactly that. His army was slow-moving, armed with tremendous siege engines and heavy cavalry, but wherever it went, it left a trail of destruction behind. By 87 BCE, he had sacked Ecbatana, once the royal seat of Cyrus the Great. All of Media fell at his feet, and that was only the beginning. Nation after nation would follow, bowing in the face of the Armenians that their imperial rulers had once so heavily subjugated: Cappadocia, Gordyene, Syria, Cilicia, and finally, Phoenicia. The latter was part of the tiny remnant of the Seleucid Empire, which had sparked the Artaxiad dynasty in the first place. It was crushed now in the face of Tigranes' onslaught.

This great king was more than just a conqueror, however. He also saw to it that his economy flourished, which helped to fuel his constant thirst for expansion as well as helping his people to thrive. The trade routes that characterized the glory of the Artaxiad dynasty were reopened and strengthened. Good relations with Babylonia made for better trade, and Armenia was mined for its abundant natural resources, with minerals like iron and salt finding their way all over the known world.

For the Armenians, a nation that had known deep oppression, it was heady stuff to be on the side of a conquering warlord. While Tigranes II seems to have treated most of the conquered nations with a fair amount of grace by allowing their kings to remain on their thrones, albeit as his vassals, Armenia was at last on the winning side. The Armenian people got to see their king riding through the countryside on one of those fiery horses that had made Armenia famous in the ancient times; Tigranes always wore a glittering tiara studded with precious stones that flashed in the sunlight like the flanks of his plunging charger, and even better, he was followed by four men on foot. These were not servants—they were subjugated kings who acted as his advisers, but they were not given the privilege of riding a horse like Tigranes was. He was the self-proclaimed king of kings, and he made sure that his vassals knew it as they ran alongside his horse in the heat and dust.

Armenia was victorious—for now. Like Alexander the Great, who was once Armenia's conqueror, Tigranes' empire would be as short-lived as it was brilliant.

Chapter 5 – Caught in the Crossfire

When Tigranes II married Cleopatra the Elder, the daughter of King Mithridates VI of Pontus, it had been a strategic move, just as the majority of royal marriages at the time were. At war with Rome, Pontus was a desperate nation, one that would be glad to ally itself even with a weakened country like Armenia. Yet becoming an ally of Pontus would prove to be Tigranes' greatest mistake.

At its height, the Armenian Empire encompassed parts of modern-day Israel, Turkey, and Iran, among others. It had fought victories against Parthia, Judea, Cilicia, and Syria, and it was ready to become an even greater kingdom. Yet one great power that Armenia had never faced in battle was Rome. The Roman Empire had been an Armenian ally for decades, even though Tigranes' rapid expansion had led to rising tensions between the two nations. Yet all that would change thanks to a bad decision Tigranes had made at the very beginning of his long and illustrious reign.

Cleopatra the Elder herself had proven to be a good enough wife for Tigranes. She wasn't the problem. However, if there was anything that Cleopatra had in abundance, it was daddy issues. Her father, Mithridates VI, was so instrumental in sparking three massive conflicts with Rome that they were named the Mithridatic Wars.

Mithridates was a particularly colorful character—and a particularly nasty king, but a glimpse into his past reveals that he had good reason to be. After his father was assassinated when Mithridates was just thirteen years old, his mother, Laodice VI, became the regent in his stead. Laodice, however, had plans to take her son's life in order to extend her own power. Mithridates fled into hiding for years before returning to cast his mother into prison and potentially assassinate his own brother, seizing power for himself. He had been fighting a war with Rome ever since.

By 75 BCE, the Third Mithridatic War was in full swing, and this time, Pontus was losing. Mithridates—by now a paranoid old man who took small doses of poison every day in a bid to build up an immunity against assassination—was forced to flee Pontus, running to the arms of his son-in-law, the mighty Tigranes the Great. Respecting the fact that Armenia had long been an ally, the Romans sent messengers to Tigranes, requesting him to surrender Mithridates to him. It would have been best for Tigranes if he had done so. Yet Mithridates, though by now useless as an ally, was still his father-in-law. Perhaps persuaded by his wife, Tigranes refused to let Mithridates go.

Furious, the Roman consulship declared war on Armenia, and Lucius Licinius Lucullus led a powerful Roman army to march on Tigranocerta, the new capital that Tigranes had ambitiously built and named after himself. Tigranes made his stand there on October 2nd, 69 BCE, but it was a fruitless one. Lucullus' men put him to flight, and the Armenian army that had recently been so successful in its conquests had no choice but to flee back toward the former capital of Artaxata. By September of the next year, Tigranes had been beaten again at Artaxata, and the winter that was rolling in over the Armenian mountaintops was one of the bleakest Tigranes had ever seen. A winter that maybe even left him nostalgic for a Parthian prison.

But by a stroke of luck, that was not the winter that Tigranes lost his empire. Lucullus' troops, plagued by disease and hesitant to suffer through another brutal Armenian winter, launched three separate mutinies over the next few months. Lucullus was recalled to Rome in 67 BCE, giving Mithridates and Tigranes both a chance to recover. Mithridates even managed to get some of his lands back, and Tigranes was able to defeat his rebellious son, Tigranes the Younger.

However, Tigranes the Younger knew that the fight with Rome was not over yet. With his tail between his legs after his father had soundly beaten his rebellion, the young man fled not to Lucullus, but to a Roman general who was rapidly engraving his name deep in the face of history: Pompey.

By 66 BCE, this statesman was already known as Pompey the Great and had enjoyed two glorious triumphs in Rome for his military achievements in Sicily and Africa. Where Lucullus failed, surely Pompey would succeed. He marched on Pontus and set Mithridates once again to flight, this time to hide in the depths of Crimea; then, Pompey turned toward Armenia. Tigranocerta was still largely destroyed, practically abandoned after Lucullus had sacked it in 68 BCE; Tigranes himself had clawed back Artaxata once Lucullus had gone and was hiding out there, and so, Pompey marched on the substitute capital, ready to raze it to the ground just like Tigranocerta.

But the loss of his former capital had broken the great Armenian king's heart. Tigranocerta had been his magnum opus, a magnificently Hellenistic city that bustled with culture and commerce. Tigranes was old by now and tired and wealthy, and he had had enough of fighting. When Pompey reached the gates of Artaxata, Tigranes decided it would be better to give up his belongings in order to make peace. He surrendered to Pompey with hardly any fighting.

Tigranes was a beaten man, but Pompey treated him largely with respect. He was allowed to keep his throne in Armenia, provided that he was more or less a client king of the Roman Empire; however, he had to surrender most of his lands, keeping only Armenia itself alongside Sophene and Gordyene. Still, Tigranes was allowed to live out his days in peace, even though the Armenian Empire was no more.

Mithridates VI, however, was not so lucky. Paralyzed by fear of the Romans and devastated by his losses in the Mithridatic Wars, the Pontic king died a slow and terrible death. First poisoning all of his wives and children, he then swallowed a hefty dose of the toxin himself. Unfortunately, possibly due to having built up so much immunity against poison over the years, the poison failed to kill him immediately. He then tried to take his life by his own sword, but his weakened hand could not drive the blade fully home. He died slowly and in horrible anguish, finally meeting his demise when his own men butchered him out of mercy.

* * * *

Following the end of the Armenian Empire, Armenia became a Roman protectorate. This was a considerable advantage for Rome, which was still embroiled in conflict with Armenia's eastern neighbor, Parthia.

The same nation that had kept Tigranes the Great captive for so many years was still at war with Rome, and since Armenia now effectively belonged to the Romans, it was compelled to provide men and resources in order to fight the Parthians.

This first occurred in the early years of the reign of Tigranes' son, Artavasdes II. Tigranes had lived out the rest of his rule in peace, dying in 55 BCE around the age of 85, and had left the kingdom to Artavasdes.

Artavasdes was keen to prove to his Roman allies that he was a worthy successor of his famous father, so when war between Rome and Parthia broke out again in 53 BCE, he was quick to volunteer reinforcements to the Roman general, Marcus Licinius Crassus. But Crassus was reluctant to share the glory or spoils with some other king. He was the commander of the most elite army in the whole world, after all—there was no need for help from some barbarian king. Crassus could defeat the Parthians all by himself, and so, he rode off with his glittering regiments in their shining armor, rejecting Artavasdes' offer.

It was one of the last mistakes that Crassus would ever make. Lured into the open by the swift horseback archers of the Parthian army, he would quickly find out that his enemy was more than just a bunch of uneducated hooligans. Those sure-footed Iranian horses could spin and run with the kind of agility that the ponderous Roman legionnaires could not face. And in the summer of 53 BCE, the Roman invasion had turned into a rout. Crassus was killed, and the Romans fled with their tails between their legs, the Parthians in hot pursuit. They made it all the way into Armenia itself, where they forced Artavasdes to join their side, marrying the Parthian crown prince to Artavasdes' sister.

For the next fifteen years, the Parthians would be left alone, allowed to gloat over their fallen enemies in Rome as they exploited the resources of Armenia. Artavasdes II was discontent, but he knew better than to try and fight off a nation that had defeated the mighty Roman Empire itself. But Rome wasn't done with Parthia, and neither was one of its most accomplished generals, Marcus Antonius, better known to history by his Shakespearean name, Mark Antony.

In 36 BCE, Antony headed into Armenia, determined to fight back against the Parthians that had given Crassus such an ignominious defeat. A wiser general than his ill-fated predecessor, Antony not only accepted Artavasdes' help: he demanded it. Artavasdes was only too glad to switch sides. His entire country had suffered the same imprisonment in which his father, Tigranes the Great, had been condemned to endure for 25 years. Thanks to stronger Roman shields and the use of the tortoise formation to guard against those horse archers, the Parthians were chased out of Armenia and back into their own country.

Armenia was liberated from Parthian rule, yet as soon as Antony had left the country in order to march on Parthia itself, Artavasdes got cold feet. He remembered seeing the defeated legionnaires of Crassus stumbling back home through Armenia, their ranks shattered, their leader killed, and he did not have the stomach to send his own men off to suffer the same fate. When Antony's Parthian campaign ended in disaster, he blamed the fickle Armenian king for failing to provide enough reinforcements. So, Antony turned the remnants of his troops around and attacked Armenia, arresting Artavasdes for treason and carrying him back off to Alexandria—the home of Antony's famous mistress, Cleopatra.

There, Antony held a mock Roman triumph, an act which Rome itself considered a defilement of a true triumph. Bringing up the rear of the grand parade was Artavasdes II and his family, bound in golden chains, booed and jeered at by the exuberant crowd. Artavasdes would never be a free man again; he would be beheaded on Cleopatra's orders within a few years, and the Artaxiad dynasty, once the heyday of Armenia, would effectively die with him. Although the dynasty would linger on until 12 CE, it was very weak, with the kings often hiding from their enemies.

* * * *

After the death of Artavasdes II and the conquest of Armenia, the country would be reduced to a kind of plaything caught in a vicious tug-of-war between Rome and Parthia. First, a Roman-backed king would find his way to the throne, then a candidate supported by Parthia, and so on, back and forth for almost a century until finally a Parthian named Tiridates was nominated to become king in the early 1st century CE.

Of course, this sparked an immediate war with Rome, once again. Emperor Nero was not amused with having a Parthian in charge of the land that was once a useful buffer zone between the warring nations, and for several years, Armenia was once again torn limb from limb in conflicts between Rome and Parthia. The fighting only ended in 63 CE when an uneasy peace was reached at last: Parthia would nominate the Armenian king, but only a Roman emperor could actually crown him. Nero begrudgingly agreed, and Tiridates I had his coronation in Rome with suitable pomp. He became the founder of the Arsacid dynasty.

The treaty between Rome and Parthia, however, was not as lasting as Tiridates' dynasty. Vespasian, who became the Roman emperor in July 69 CE, was quick to annex Armenia entirely. Under Roman protection, Armenia was reduced to a province of the empire, but nonetheless, it had a brief period of peace at last.

After centuries of warfare, Parthia itself was also starting to decline in importance. By the reign of Hadrian in the early 2nd century, Parthia appears to have been tired of fighting with Rome, and Armenia became more trouble than it was worth for the great old empire. Hadrian gave the country its independence, and for the first time since Tigranes the Great, Armenia was free once again.

As usual, its freedom would be short-lived. Another power was rising up in the ancient world. And the Parthians were nothing compared to this new Persian force.

Chapter 6 – Illumination

Lucius Verus was the emperor of Rome—a title that he found most troublesome.

Raised in the house of Antonius Pius, Lucius had had nothing but good role models to follow growing up: Antonius Pius was well known for being one of Rome's most astute emperors, while Lucius's adoptive brother, Marcus Aurelius, would go down in history as a philosopher emperor. Marcus was a Stoic, a man whose belief in moderation and simplicity was deep and steady. Lucius was anything but. It had been an annoying interlude in his life of opulence and constant partying when Antonius had died in 161 and left the Roman Empire in the hands of his two adopted sons, but Marcus had luckily taken up most of Lucius' slack, allowing him to do whatever he pleased.

That was until that pesky Parthian king, Vologases IV, marched on Armenia and set up one of his generals as its king. He had been waiting for Antonius to die, and it was less than a year since Marcus and Lucius had become emperors of Rome. Marcus knew he had to stay where he was and consolidate his power, so he sent Lucius to deal with the Parthian problem.

How irritating, Lucius thought. Never mind—perhaps there was fun to be had in the Middle East.

* * * *

Despite Lucius Verus' lackadaisical attitude, he had talented generals, and most of them were quite relieved that he elected to stay at his new resort in Syria instead of getting his hands dirty. Generals like Marcus Statius Priscus and Gaius Avidius Cassius were able to win yet another fight with Parthia over Armenia, reinstating the Arsacid dynasty in 166 CE. Lucius, who had never even seen Armenia, bestowed upon himself the title of Armeniacus to celebrate "his" victory.

It was the last time that a Parthian would sit on the Armenian throne. The Parthian Empire, which had been a thorn in Rome's side for five hundred years, was falling into decline. It had stood against the might of Rome for so many centuries, but the Romans would not be the ones to defeat it; instead, it was the Parthian nobility themselves that staged an uprising and overthrew their king. Ardashir I, a former king of Persis, killed the Parthian king, Artabanus IV, in 224. He claimed to be a descendant of Sasan, a legendary hero, and thus, the dynasty he founded was named the Sasanid dynasty. It would rule over Persia for over 400 years, and Ardashir was the first to call his country by the name it bears today: Iran. He also took the same title that Tigranes the Great of the Armenian Empire had born, *Shahanshah*, or "king of kings."

The fall of Parthia, an empire that had devastated Armenia for so many centuries, was only a brief respite for the Armenian people. They had not asked to be involved in half a millennium of conflict, caught as they were between the two great powers of the ancient world, and yet their suffering was not over. In 252, the Sasanids attacked. They feared that the Armenian Arsacid kings, who had blood ties through Vonones I to the old Parthian royalty, would make an attempt to claim the Persian throne. They invaded, and Rome retaliated. Once again, Armenia was reduced to a battlefield that was not respected by either one of the nations at war on those windswept highlands.

In the very same year that the Sasanids first invaded, Ardashir's son, Shapur, ordered one of his minions—a man known as Anak—to assassinate the royal family of Armenia. Anak butchered the queen, and the king, Khosrov II, was killed soon afterward. The only remaining male heir to the Armenian throne was a two-year-old boy named Tiridates. His relatives were quick to smuggle him to safety as his country was ripped apart without a king to lead it. Meanwhile, the remaining Armenian nobility captured and executed Anak and his whole family—except for a little boy named Gregory. And these two children, who had suffered such a deep and mutual tragedy, would change Armenian history forever.

* * * *

Tiridates had been raised in a Roman court. Despite the fact that Rome's argument with Armenia had caused the country so much grief over the centuries, Rome remained Armenia's key ally, and considering that the Persians had killed his family, Tiridates had nowhere else to turn. He was a helpless little toddler when he was brought to the great city, and he would remain there for the rest of his childhood.

But once he was a grown man, Tiridates knew that he could not hide in the safety of Rome forever. He had to go back to the country that he did not remember. The country that was his ancestral homeland.

The country that needed him to rise up as king.

When Roman Emperor Marcus Aurelius expelled the Sasanids from Armenia in 270, the twenty-year-old Tiridates saw his chance. He traveled back to Armenia, and the people rallied around him, helping him to keep back the relentless tide of Persian invaders. The Sasanid Empire fell into a state of civil war, and Tiridates was able not only to strengthen his borders but also to win parts of Assyria for his army.

By 298 CE, Tiridates III had unified his entire country, and he had found a powerful and close ally in the emperor that had grown up in the city alongside him: Diocletian. Having murdered a usurper with his own hands, Diocletian had come to power in 284 CE and supported Tiridates in his conquests. They were united in a common thread of hatred. Tiridates, with only traumatic memories of his murdered family, hated the Sasanids. And Diocletian, strongly influenced by his right-hand man Galerius, hated the Christians. He would be made famous for being one of the harshest persecutors of Christianity in the history of the Roman Empire.

Tiridates, for his part, was different from most Armenians in that he did not practice Zoroastrianism with the same dedication as the rest of his people. The ancient religion had been part and parcel of Armenian culture for around eight hundred years, but it was still a Persian religion, and Tiridates hated it. Instead, he was a pagan, practicing the old polytheistic faith that had been in Armenia long before Zoroaster ever walked the earth. But there was a new player in the religious game of Armenia, too. Ever since the mid-1st century CE, when Thaddeus and Bartholomew—two of Jesus' original disciples—brought the Gospels to Armenia, the people had been practicing early Christianity. And despite the looming threat of persecution from Diocletian, Armenians held steadily to this new faith.

This faith had found footing in Cappadocia, too, where Christian schools had been flourishing. And in one of these schools, a little boy had grown up, a boy who bore the burden of a bloodstained family conscience on his shoulders. His name was Grigor Lusavorich, although he would go down in history as Gregory the Illuminator. And he felt profoundly guilty for the fact that his father, Anak, had murdered the Armenian royal family.

Gregory had been improbably rescued after his whole family was executed and taken to Cappadocia, where he could have lived a quietly anonymous life if he had chosen. Instead, spurred on by his shame and a desire to right his father's wrongs, Gregory traveled to Armenia as a young man and was given a position in Tiridates' court at Vagharshapat as a palace functionary. Every day, he lived and worked in the very shadow of the man who had grown up a bitter orphan because of what his father had done. And every day, Gregory clung to the faith that was the only reason he could believe he was somehow forgiven. That he was somehow redeemed.

That faith had changed his life. And it would change Armenian history.

* * * *

Anahit was the pagan goddess of healing and fertility, and in Tiridates' eyes, she was the glory of his nation. Depicted as a beautiful young woman, Anahit had bronze and golden statues all over Armenia, and her cult had been flourishing for four hundred years. Tiridates worshiped her wholeheartedly, and his entire retinue was expected to do the same—including Gregory, the secret Christian.

It was likely a bright day in spring or summer, as it was the day of a religious ceremony dedicated to the golden goddess whose gleaming statue shone in the court of Eriza, where Tiridates had made his pilgrimage to pay his respects to the mother goddess. His retinue carried wreaths of flowers, ready to lay them down as sacrifices at the feet of Anahit. One by one, Tiridates' servants obediently did so until only one young man was left. Annoyed that he had not taken the initiative, Tiridates ordered him to lay down his wreath.

And Gregory did the unthinkable. He defied the king.

Taking a stand, the young servant refused to lay his garland of flowers at the golden feet of the statue of Anahit. He told the king and everyone watching that he did not practice polytheism the way they did—he was a Christian, and he would rather die than deny his faith.

The move was one of not only religious but also political significance. Tiridates had no choice but to deal harshly with this young man; no one, especially not some lowly servant, could be allowed to get away with defying the king of Armenia. Gregory was in trouble even before Tiridates found out that he was the last surviving member of Anak's family. Nothing could have pacified the king in his burst of royal rage. He ordered Gregory to be cast into Khor Virap, the "bottomless pit," a dark and terrifying underground dungeon from which no one returned alive. This likely occurred around 288 CE if the legend is accurate.

The legend of Gregory and Tiridates III grows murky with the years, and it is difficult to separate fact from fiction, but the story goes that Gregory languished in Khor Virap for thirteen terrible years. He only survived thanks to a kind old lady who used to bring him scraps of bread; Tiridates, meanwhile, ordered the Christians to be persecuted, a move that would soon be echoed by his friend Diocletian.

History is sure that Tiridates continued to expand Armenia, establishing it back into an echo of its former glory, a feat for which he would become known as Tiridates the Great. Diocletian was instrumental in assisting him. By 299, the Sasanids had been resoundingly defeated and cast out into their own country, and Armenia was no longer a mere province of the Roman Empire. Instead, it was a protectorate and had been granted more independence than it had enjoyed in a long time. Satisfied with his work, Diocletian returned to Rome to persecute Christianity in his own realm.

By that time, Gregory had been in the ghastly dungeon for eleven long years. He would languish there for two more years before a legendary disease began to afflict the king. Tiridates was struck with what was then known as lycanthropy; he began to behave "like a wild boar," stumbling around as if lost in the palace and its grounds, his mind leaving him. None of the pagan priests or Armenian physicians could do anything for him.

His relief would come from the unlikeliest quarter. Khosrovidukht, Tiridates' sister and fellow survivor of Anak's assassination, had a dream that Gregory was still alive and that he was the only one capable of curing Tiridates' affliction. It was a long shot, but she knew that she had to try. She retrieved a weak and sickly Gregory from the prison and brought him to Tiridates, and when he laid his hands on the raving and ailing king, the disease lifted from him miraculously. It was enough to cause Tiridates to convert on the spot. He became a Christian, and seeking a means with which to defy the Sasanids—who were still deeply faithful pagans and Zoroastrians—he made Armenia the first country to officially adopt Christianity as its state religion in 301.

For his actions, Gregory was canonized. He is known to history as Saint Gregory the Illuminator, the patron saint of Armenia.

Chapter 7 – Immortals and War Elephants

Illustration II: The Battle of Avarayr, as imagined by Eduard Isabekyan

The fact that Tiridates III had become a Christian, a religion that was being heavily persecuted by Rome at the time, did not put a stop to religious persecution in Armenia. Sadly, instead of stopping the practice altogether, Tiridates simply switched sides. He was utterly determined to see Christianity become Armenia's dominant religion—and not simply for pious motives. Instead, Tiridates saw Christianity as an act of defiance against the hated Sasanids, and so, he also saw every person who failed to worship the way he did as a threat to his throne and a potential ally of Persia.

Pagans, those who practiced the same polytheism that Tiridates once so fervently had, were subject to the same brutal treatment that the Christian Armenians had suffered prior to 301 CE. Temples and statues were destroyed, and many historical texts by pagans were burned, leaving a great black hole in Armenian history thanks to the wrath of the king.

The ancient world was experiencing a seismic shift when it came to religion. The polytheism and Zoroastrianism that had dominated the world was living on borrowed time. Only a decade after Tiridates was baptized, the Roman emperor Constantine converted, too. His move of the empire's capital to Byzantium marked the beginning of a rift of ancient Rome, splitting the empire into two: the Western Roman Empire, with its capital in Rome, and the Byzantine or Eastern Roman Empire, with its capital eventually finding its way to Constantinople—modern-day Istanbul.

Despite strenuous resistance from the pagans, which eventually culminated in a pitched battle of pagan forces against the might of Tiridates' army and ended in inevitable victory for Tiridates, the king succeeded in turning Armenia into a predominantly Christian nation. Gregory, of course, was its first archbishop. Armenia had to find its way now in a world that was rapidly shifting and changing as antiquity began to blend quietly into the Middle Ages.

The everyday Armenian was no longer allowed to have idols in his home or pray to his ancestral gods. He could no longer mourn in the traditional ways, which often took place in the form of lamenting dances that involved actually cutting one's own skin. Nor could a man marry several wives; marriage, formerly a loose arrangement that had little to do with the law, became a more formal institution, recognizable to modern-day marriages. The old rituals were dead, and a new world was being ushered in, one that many Armenians found repugnant. However, particularly supported by Gregory, charitable institutions were also springing up around Armenia thanks to its Christianization. These included hospitals and orphanages, as well as special homes for lepers.

By the end of the 4th century, Armenia had become mostly Christian, with the final pockets of pagan resistance being weeded out. The Western Roman Empire had largely lost interest in the little nation, but the Byzantine Empire still faced the Sasanids across the bruised buffer zone formed by Armenia. Just like Rome and Parthia, the Byzantine Empire and the Sasanids played a bloody tug-of-war with Armenia, disregarding the lives of its innocent citizens. Despite Tiridates' fervent war on the Sasanids, by the end of the century, the Armenian kings were more or less client kings for the Sasanids. They were barely able to make any choices without Persian approval.

The start of the 5th century, however, ushered in a time of hope—a so-called Golden Age and the swansong of the Arsacid dynasty. This time was carried on the feet of Saint Mesrop Mashtots, a monk with a powerful vision to change the lives of the people of his country.

The original Holy Bible had been written predominantly in Hebrew and Greek. As Christianity spread wildly across the world, the Bible began to be translated so that more and more common people would be able to read it. Jerome of Rome was one of the first, translating the entire Bible into Latin in the late 4th century; the Goths, a Germanic tribe, were hot on his heels and translated the Bible into their now-extinct language, Gothic. Armenia's rising Christian population was clamoring for a Bible of their own, one that even the common man could understand. Educated Armenians could all likely speak both Greek and Latin, but commoners spoke the various dialects of Armenian.

The only trouble with translating the Bible into Armenian was that it more or less failed to exist as a written language. Despite the fact that the language had been spoken for thousands of years—ever since Urartu—it had seldom been used for writing. Mesrop was determined to change that, as he wanted to spread the Gospels across the kingdom by making its holy text more accessible to all Armenians in their own tongue.

Mesrop had been born a Mamikonian. This noble Armenian family was rapidly proving itself to be almost as powerful as the Arsacids themselves; their members were educated and important in Armenian politics, being brought close to the king. Mesrop was no exception. A gifted linguist from the start, he worked alongside King Khosrov IV, writing laws or edicts for him. But Mesrop's heart was not in politics. He wanted to dedicate himself to a humbler life, one of piety and service, and so, he became a monk and joined a monastery around 395 when he was in his thirties. A few years earlier, Khosrov had been deposed by dissatisfied Sasanids. They made another member of the Arsacid family, Vramshapuh, king in his stead.

That is not to say that Mesrop faded from history. Far from it. Allying himself with Isaac the Great, the archbishop of Armenia, Mesrop expressed his determination to turn Armenian into a written language that the people could use to read the Scripture and worship. Despite the fact that this was a risky move for a king so deeply under the Sasanids' thumb, Vramshapuh agreed to lend his assistance, too, in the form of support and funding. By 405 CE, Mesrop had designed a 36-letter Armenian alphabet uniquely suited to this ancient language. Together with Isaac and a Greek named Rufanos, Mesrop spent the next five years translating the first Armenian Bible, known as the Mesropic Bible.

The invention of the Armenian alphabet and the spread of the Bible in the native Armenian language marked the beginning of a Golden Age for Christian literature. Armenia had, at last, a voice in the realm of writing, and written works abounded in the language. It began to seem as though Armenia had a place in the world after all, despite continuous oppression from the Sasanids. But this rise in Armenian national identity did not sit well with their enemies in Persia. Armenians were starting to realize that they were unique, that they were their own people with their own religion and language, something very separate from the Sasanids. This pride and knowledge were dangerous, and it would have to be stopped. In just a few short years, the lives of everyday Armenians would change once again, as disaster was on the horizon.

* * * *

The Sasanid army came across the plain of Avarayr like something from Vardan Mamikonian's worst nightmares.

The commander of the Armenian people could trace his lineage back to St. Gregory, and he felt like he now knew an inkling of the fear that his ancestor had suffered in the depths of Khor Virap. And with good reason. Vardan was looking up at an army that had struck fear into the heart of Alexander the Great himself, an army that had become a legend for its fearsome qualities. He knew that even its appearance on the horizon was sending shivers down the spines of his largely inexperienced, disorganized band of rebels. Trying to keep up their spirits, he called back to them that God was with them. That whatever happened on this day, they would live or die for the Lord they served, on their own terms and not bowing to Sasanid demands.

It was just enough encouragement to keep the Armenian army rooted to the spot as they watched the heavy infantry marching toward them, their movements so synchronized that they appeared to be almost robotic. Their heavy shields were held in front of them, spears slicing the sky above them. The appearance of their infantry would have been intimidating enough, even if Vardan had not known that they were so indomitable as to be known as the Immortals. Wherever one of these infantrymen fell—and despite their light armor, they did not fall often—another would be ready to take his place. Fighting an Immortal was like fighting something you could not kill. He never seemed to be dead for long; there was always another, fresher, stronger one at the end of your blade once you had cut him down.

But the Immortals were only the half of it. Close on their heels, slow and lumbering under the weight of their enormous strength, came the war elephants. Murmurs of terror rippled through Vardan's ranks, and even he felt an insistent disquiet at the sight of these tremendous creatures. The foremost one paused, raised its trunk in the air as if to scent out the enemy. It threw open its ears, making it seem even bigger, and shook its head. The long white tusks caught the sunlight, and Vardan remembered all that he had learned about the war elephants that Persia brought from India. The towers on their backs were filled with armed men, but that was not what made the elephants dangerous. They were not simply beasts of burden. They were weapons in their own right; trained to trample and impale their enemies, they could crush a troop of cavalry, swiping a horse aside with a single blow of their tusks as if it was little more than a fly.

And Vardan Mamikonian was still standing his ground on the plain of Avarayr on this once-quiet morning of June 2nd, 451, the stillness of the day shattered now by the sound of the marching Immortals and the trumpeting of the war elephants, even though he only had 66,000 men at his command. Even though he knew that this was fruitless, as they were facing the mighty Sasanids with what amounted to little more than a bunch of hopeful revolutionaries. There were some experienced Armenian fighters in his army, but Vardan knew that the bulk of his men were made up of ordinary people. Ordinary people who wanted to defend their way of life and their right to worship the God they loved. Their only hope was for the Byzantine reinforcements that Vardan had begged for to arrive in time—if they arrived at all.

It had all started in 428 CE. Having deposed a series of unsatisfactory kings, the Sasanids were growing testy with the Arsacid dynasty. The growing rise of Christianity was also perceived as exactly what Tiridates had wanted it to be: a threat to Persian authority. The Armenians were beginning to believe in a power even bigger than the Persians, and unlike Zoroastrianism, this power could not be wielded by Persian hands. It gave them hope, and hope was dangerous to the Persian king, Bahram V, for whom Armenia was a vital foothold in the continual war with the Byzantine Empire.

Bahram was not the only one who was concerned with the increasingly strong sense of identity pervading the Armenian psyche. The Persian nobility involved in governing Armenia was beginning to worry, too, enjoying their cushy lives under Sasanid protection while hating this new faith. They petitioned Bahram to depose the last Arsacid king, Artaxias IV, which he did in 428. Armenia was now little more than a Persian province.

For the Armenian nobility, including Vardan and his friends, this was no great trouble. Armenia had been ruled by Persia for decades, after all—the Persians protected them and did not oppress them too harshly. Artaxias had been little more than a figurehead anyways. But all that would change after Bahram died.

Bahram's successor, Yazdegerd II, was not the ruler that Bahram had been. Instead, he was determined to subjugate Armenia, not only physically but also spiritually. Yazdegerd could not care less what god the Armenians worshiped, as long as it was not their own god, one that was unique to them. One that gave them that dangerous identity. He petitioned them to join the Church of the East, from which the Armenians had seceded long ago, or better yet, to convert to the same religion that he followed himself, Zoroastrianism. But the Armenians held firm, and Yazdegerd grew tired of asking nicely. He sent his Zoroastrian priests into Armenia, backed by the military, and ordered them to destroy the Christian churches and build Zoroastrian temples instead.

The Armenian Christians found themselves being oppressed and persecuted once more, as the religion in which they found their identity was stripped cruelly away. Vardan Mamikonian was chief among those who were angered by this turn of events. He had once sympathized with the Persians, but those days were over now. He would lead his people to the religious freedom they deserved—or die trying.

Sadly, history would prove to favor the latter. Vardan's 66,000-strong band of fighters did not stand a chance against the Sasanids, of whom there were more than 300,000, with some of them being Armenians who favored Persian rule. The battle was brief, bloody, and decisive. Vardan and his men were butchered on that plain, and the elephants trampled their blood into the dirt.

* * * *

The Battle of Avarayr was a devastating defeat for Christian Armenia. However, even with Vardan dead, the Mamikonians still refused to give up. Vardan's nephew, Vahan Mamikonian, continued to fight against the Sasanids. This time avoiding a pitched battle, Vahan fought a long and grueling guerrilla war that nonetheless succeeded in wearing down Sasanid resolve to impose Zoroastrianism. In 484 CE, the Nvarsak Treaty finally realized the late Vardan's vision: to allow Armenians to practice whatever religion they chose.

For his part, Vardan was made St. Vardan, and he remains a cultural hero to Armenians to this day. One cannot help but wonder how things would have turned out differently at the Battle of Avarayr if the Byzantine reinforcements had arrived the way the Byzantine emperor, Marcian, had promised. But relations between Armenia and the Byzantine Empire were far from over. An emperor with Armenian blood in his veins was going to take the throne, and he was going to be an Armenian hero in a new and even more gruesome war, a war that would last to the modern day.

Chapter 8 – An Armenian Emperor

Despite the fact that Armenia had been little more than a disposable battleground to the Byzantine Empire for centuries, the tide was changing. Armenia would not be a mere pawn to Byzantium forever, not the way that it had always been to Rome. Armenian influence would grow in the Byzantine Empire, and it would change the importance of this bruised and bloodied country in history.

A new age was dawning. The ancient time was fading into the shadows; the years governed by Persia and Media, by Rome and Macedonia, were almost over. Yet the time of conquering warlords was nowhere near its end, and as the world began to shift into the Middle Ages, two mighty powers would emerge from the chaos. Powers that clash to this very day—and powers that would never clash harder than in Armenia.

But all that was centuries in the future. For now, Armenia's influence in the Byzantine Empire was growing. At first, Armenia had been to the Byzantines and Sasanids just what it had been to the Romans and Parthians, divided up twice in the late 4th and early 5th centuries as if it was little more than a cake and its people were mere decorations. Things had been made worse in 451 when Byzantine relief failed to save the Christian Armenians at Avarayr. Instead, while the Armenians were suffering their terrible defeat, the Byzantines were holding the Council of Chalcedon. The failure of the Armenian Church to be at the council resulted in a rift that divided the Eastern Orthodox Church from the Armenian Church, a rift that still exists to this day.

Yet even though the Byzantines treated the Armenians as being theologically inferior, they certainly had use of them in their armies. By the end of the 5th century, the Armenians from the Byzantine-controlled (and smaller) portion of Armenia made up the bulk of the army, and they had made such a name for themselves that the palace guards were handpicked from among their ranks. Eager to seek the prosperity that the Byzantine Empire offered, Armenians flocked to its nearby capital, which was then Byzantium. It has been said that the Armenian effect on Byzantine history has been vastly underestimated as Armenian military leaders worked their way up to fame and success in Byzantium.

Entering the 6th century, Armenia was still divided. The largest portion of its historical territory still belonged to the Sasanids, but in 582, all that was about to change.

Ever since the year 562, Byzantium and Persia had arrived at a forced treaty. Both were struggling with other invaders, and both knew that they could no longer afford to challenge one another and protect their own borders. An uneasy peace began, but Armenians in the Sasanid part of the country were unhappy with these arrangements. Byzantine Armenia was far more prosperous than Sasanid Armenia; added to that, while the Sasanid Armenians were more or less free to practice Christianity, the Sasanids were still Zoroastrians. If the Armenians had to have overlords, they wanted them to be Christians. In 571, the peace was broken when Armenia revolted, and Emperor Justin II of the Byzantine Empire sent an army to fight the Sasanids on the Armenians' behalf.

It was a thrilling day for the Armenians when the Persian governor was driven out of his home at Dvin, an almost poetic victory in the light of the defeat at Avarayr more than 150 years earlier; their commander was named Vardan II Mamikonian, and he achieved what his namesake could not. But while the Armenians were doing well, the Byzantines fared poorly. The important city of Dara fell to the Persians in 573, a blow that utterly shattered Emperor Justin II. He suffered a mental breakdown and abdicated a year later, leaving the Byzantine throne to his general, Tiberius. The old general ruled for a further four years after Justin's death in 578 as Tiberius II Constantine, and upon his death, the Byzantine-Persian war was still raging. He knew on his deathbed that he would have to hand over the war to a young man who had proven himself in battle against the Persians, and that man was Mauricius Flavius Tiberius, who was crowned Emperor Maurice.

Maurice had witnessed firsthand the devastation that Persia had wrought in Armenia, as well as the abundant natural and human resources in the country. One of his first moves as emperor, after he was crowned in 582, was to renew the war on Persia. The bitter and bloody fight would continue until 591, and it was not the Byzantines' prowess that saved Armenia. Once again, it was trouble within Persia itself. Civil war broke out there in 589, and one of the opposing kings fighting to claim the throne, Khosrow II, sought Maurice's aid. In exchange for putting Khosrow on the throne, Maurice won back Armenia for Byzantium. This was a victory for the Armenians, but it was even more so a boon for Byzantium, as now there were even more Armenians available to fill up the ranks of the army with seasoned fighters.

Saving Armenia was not Maurice's only accomplishment as emperor. Over the next twenty years of his reign, Maurice succeeded in scraping back together a fragmented and shattered empire that was on the brink of collapse. His leadership shaped the Byzantine Empire into a force that would be able to withstand the breaking waves of time, far outlasting its western cousin. But for all the good that he had done, Maurice would die gruesomely. He had never treated his soldiers particularly well, spending his money frugally on them while focusing on other areas in his empire, and in 602, they revolted against him led by a man named Phocas.

Phocas was a centurion in Maurice's army, and he was a fairly good military commander—as well as a rather brutal human being. He succeeded in rallying the army to overthrow Maurice and claimed the title of emperor for himself, becoming one of history's most legendary usurpers and tyrants. Maurice did not have to live long with the humiliation of being defeated by a mere army officer, as he and his six sons were slaughtered by Phocas in 602.

For the next eight years, Phocas' rule would rain terror upon the subjects of the Byzantine Empire, and the Armenians were no exception. A zealous persecutor of Christianity, Phocas made the lives of most of his subjects fairly miserable. Armenia found itself fighting to defend the Byzantine border from a vengeful Khosrow, who was determined to overthrow the man who had usurped his ally, and in the war that followed, it was the Armenians who would be cut down by the thousands as the Sasanids once again trampled bloodily over their country.

Discontent spread wildly across the whole of the empire. Riots erupted in Byzantium as even the nobles started to rebel against Phocas, who had become nothing short of a tyrant. And in Armenia, there was little hope. They had been badly treated by the Sasanids, so they had looked for salvation from Byzantium, but now the Byzantines were treating them just as badly.

There was no Maurice coming to save them this time. But there was someone with Armenian blood in his veins. Someone determined to save his ethnic homeland and the whole of the ailing empire.

That hero was Heraclius. The son of an Armenian governor, although he had grown up in Carthage as a Greek, Heraclius was well aware that the blood in his veins originated on the highlands of Armenia. It was his Armenian father, aware of the plight of all the

Byzantines, that first stirred up his heart against Phocas. And in 610, eight years after Phocas usurped the throne, Heraclius and his fleet sailed forth to Byzantium. Their plan was to lay siege to the capital in a large-scale revolt, but it was hardly necessary. By then, there was scarcely a man left in Byzantium who would fight on Phocas' behalf. According to some sources, by the time Heraclius reached the city walls, Phocas had been butchered by his own nobles. His corpse—robbed of the arms, legs, and head—was handed over to Heraclius as a gruesome trophy, and his head was carried around the streets of the city he had terrorized on a spear.

It is difficult to comprehend a more picture-perfect hero to the Christian population of the empire than Heraclius. A sturdy man in his thirties, Heraclius even looked the part; tall and powerfully built, he was a picture of magnificence in his gleaming armor, topped with a mop of hair so deeply golden that it might as well have been spun from the sunshine. With Maurice and his heir dead, he was considered the savior of Byzantium, the driving force that had spurred the nobles to revolt at last. He was promptly crowned emperor and was promptly faced with the Persian problem.

Phocas had made little attempt to stand against the Sasanids, who had wrought destruction and heartache on the empire, starting in the Holy Land that was so precious to the hearts of a majorly Christian populace. The Sasanids overwhelmed cities as integral to the faith as Damascus and Jerusalem, and most abominable of all—in the Christian Armenians' eyes—they carried off the True Cross from Jerusalem. Of course, they had also reclaimed Armenia and continued their persecution of its citizens. The Armenians were besieged on every side, both physically and spiritually.

Heraclius' first priority was to end the war that Maurice had worked so hard to stop. He rode out against the Sasanids, and at first, he experienced one of the worst times of hardship that Byzantium ever suffered. Constantinople was besieged, and Egypt was lost, sparking famine throughout the empire as it was cut off from its major supply of grain. Despite losing the faith of his people as a result of his failures (and marrying his cousin, Martina), Heraclius managed to rally. In 622, he attacked the Persians in Armenia, and this time, they would be driven out for good. Heraclius, for all his other failings, did succeed in saving his homeland from the Sasanids. And it would be the last time that those Sasanids would ever occupy it.

Persia had been terrorizing Armenia ever since the days of Parthia. But a new power was about to rise up—a power that would overwhelm the Sasanids and, ultimately, prove to be the greatest threat of all to the Armenian people.

Chapter 9 – Crusader State

Illustration III: The ruins of Ani

By the time Heraclius had finished his work, he had become unpopular among his own people for the tribulations that his war on Persia had put them through, but at least the Byzantines had been victorious. The Sasanids, whose empire was in decline, had been forced back into Persia, and peace was reached at last.

Meanwhile, all the way in Arabia, a tremendous shift was about to change the course of history, creating ripples that are still powerfully felt today. Islam was on the rise.

Before the 7th century, Islam, as we know it, did not exist. It was only in the year 610 CE —the same year that Heraclius was defeating Phocas in Byzantium—that the Prophet Muhammad of Arabia, according to Islamic tradition, received visions from the angel Gabriel. Gabriel gave him a series of commands, inspiring Muhammad to begin preaching what he called the "true religion" around 613. His following grew with tremendous speed. Muhammad's ideas were not all alien; in fact, the new religion he was preaching shared many concepts and even respected prophets prevalent in Christianity and Judaism. They were readily accepted by many of his fellow Arabians, and by the time of Muhammad's death in 632, Islam was more than just the following of a single prophet. It was a religion in its own right.

As it is today, the majority of the original Muslims were ordinary peace-loving people who wanted what everyone in the history of the world has wanted: food, family, peace, purpose, and an understanding of the world around them. They wanted something to believe in. But sadly, even then, a group of radicals began to commit violence in the name of Islam. The first holy war had begun.

Muhammad's body was hardly cold when his followers, whom by now had established the Arab Caliphate, began to seek to extend their lands. While Muhammad had sent letters to the rulers of various powers—including Byzantium and Persia—his successors favored a more direct approach, one that would give them more wealth and glory. By 642, ten years after Muhammad's death, the caliph of the time, Umar, had set his sights on Sasanid Persia. The power that had stood up to Byzantium for four hundred years was weakened now, and it did not stand a chance against the strong hordes of the Arabs.

With the Sasanids gone, the Arab armies were able to turn on their neighbors, the Armenians. For the first time in history, Armenia—now almost entirely Christian—was facing an Islamic foe. And it would not be the last.

* * * *

As the Arsacid dynasty had fallen, the city of Dvin had risen again. The capital of Armenia since the first Persian *marzpan*, or overlord, had taken hold of the city, Dvin was ideally situated for commerce and agriculture. Its stern walls were surrounded by luxurious green fields and the richest pasture that the country could offer. Those pastures had once been covered in the glittering shapes of grazing horses. The earth had once rung with the thunder of their hooves as the fleet-footed youngsters chased one another back and forth across the grass, biting and bucking and playing, just like their ancestors had done thousands of years ago when their athleticism first made Armenia famous. Men and women had fed, groomed, ridden those horses across the wide-flung grasslands and on the craggy mountaintops just about forty miles away from Mount Ararat. But now, the fields were trampled, the grass crushed underneath the feet of camels. The walls had been torn down, and the horses and the men that had loved them lay butchered in the very streets.

Sources differ slightly on how exactly it came about that the Arabs defeated Armenia, but it is known that there was defeat and that it was absolutely devastating. Even when Rome and Parthia, or Byzantium and Persia, had squabbled back and forth across the country, it had been because Armenia was valuable to them. They may have seen the people as mere cattle to fill the ranks of their armies, but at least they were useful cattle. The Armenians had seen so much war, but according to a contemporary Armenian historian named Bishop Sebeos, they had never seen anything like the Muslims.

Ever since the beginning of the Muslim conquest of Persia—around 639—the Arabs had been raiding the borders of Armenia, taking little chunks out of the country but were never quite successful. But with the Persians subjugated by 642, they could turn their full attention on Armenia. And even the seasoned Armenian armies, backed up by Byzantines when Heraclius' grandson, Constans II, was able to spare a few men, would soon find out that they were no match for the blazing wrath of the Arab armies.

Sebeos was an eyewitness to the terrible fate of Dvin. The city was not merely besieged; it was ransacked. According to this Armenian historian, the Arabs attacked it "with fire and sword," killing and capturing all that lived and burning everything else. By the time the Arabs were done with it, Dvin was no longer the bustling capital of the Armenia that Heraclius had rescued. With 12,000 people dead and 35,000 more (mostly women and children) taken captive, Dvin was utterly destroyed.

* * * *

The sad fate of Dvin was not the end of Armenia's troubles with the Arab Caliphate. After sacking Dvin, the Arabs pulled back for a while, returning in 643 with an even more devastating attack; this time, the Armenian governor, Theodore Rshtuni, managed to push them back. Eventually, however, Rshtuni submitted to Arabic rule. For the next several decades, Armenia was passed back and forth between the Arabs and the Byzantines. Anytime that Armenia submitted to the Arabs, it was attacked by the Byzantines; when it swore allegiance to the Byzantines again in 656, the Arab caliph murdered almost two thousand Armenian hostages. Armenia was once again between a rock and a hard place.

The rest of the 7th and 8th centuries were spent more or less under Arab rule. When Arabs attempted to impose Islam on the general population, rebellions were sparked, but none of them ever gained enough ground to fully throw off their shackles. Like Vardan Mamikonian on the battlefield of Avarayr, thousands of Armenians perished defending their right to worship as they pleased. Nonetheless, the Arabs soon realized that it was impossible to force the entire populace to convert to Islam. Despite the fact that Armenia had not been independent for centuries, its people still had a ferocious independence when it came to their beliefs, and they would not be dictated to when it came to that.

By the end of the 9th century, a noble family of Armenians had risen from the general chaos of the country as being the most powerful: the Bagratunis. A shift of power, with the Khazars (a powerful group of Turkic nomads living in modern-day Russia) allying themselves with Byzantium, had left the Arab Caliphate far more cautious than in its early days. Armenia was once again providing a buffer between two warring powers—the Christian Byzantine Empire and the Muslim Arab Caliphate—and with their borders and armies run ragged by warfare, both were content to allow Armenia to become a no man's land. For the first time since the days of the ancient Romans, Armenia became an independent kingdom in 885.

The architect of this new independence was Ashot I. Already in his sixties by the time he actually became king, Ashot had been fighting for his country ever since he was a young man—and not only with the sword. An adept diplomat, it was Ashot who managed to convince both the Byzantines and the Arabs that an independent Armenia would only be useful to both of them. This was confirmed in 885 when each of the two clashing empires sent messengers to Ashot bearing a crown. So, with two crowns and a skilled wit, Ashot became the first king of the Bagratid Kingdom of Armenia.

And for 160 years, Armenia would flourish once again as a free country. Its rulers were wise enough, on the whole, not to pursue unnecessary conflicts with other countries, even as the major powers of the time were clashing violently with one another, and so, Armenia gained a reputation for being as peace-loving as it was diverse. Its population included both Muslims and Christians, and at the height of the Bagratid Kingdom's power, its capital city, Ani, became known as the "city of a thousand and one churches." A bustling center of culture, arts, and commerce, Ani was a jewel of the Middle Ages, a rare cultural gem to be found on the highlands of one of the oldest countries of them all.

But the glory days of Ani and of the Bagratid Kingdom of Armenia would be even more numbered than those of Urartu or the glorious kingdom over which Tigranes had reigned. A new power—also Muslim but not Arabic, this time—was growing in the region: the Seljuk Turks. Originating in modern-day Kazakhstan, the Seljuks were a warlike band of Muslim Turks bent on conquering their world, and they were supported by their fellow Muslims, the Arabs. First emerging in the early 11th century, the Seljuks conquered Persia and Iraq. Armenia was the logical next step.

Yet it was not the Seljuks who eventually tolled the death bell for this ancient kingdom. Instead, it was their former allies, the Byzantines, who ended the Bagratuni Dynasty and captured Armenia in 1045.

The day of the Seljuks was coming, however. The Byzantines would only hold on to Armenia for nineteen years before the Seljuk Turks attacked in 1064. Ani, once one of the busiest and most beautiful metropolises on the face of the Caucasus, the beloved center of Armenian culture and home to more than a hundred thousand people, fell to the Turks that same year. For the first time, Armenia was in the grip of the Turkish people, and that grip would last for many devastating centuries.

* * * *

Still, the Armenian people refused to let go of their Christian faith. And luckily for some of them, there were many Europeans who also felt compelled to cling to it—and to defend it, regardless of the cost in human life. These men were the Crusaders.

As a ferocious war erupted across the whole world, pitting Christian forces against the Muslims, many Armenians fled their own homeland. An exodus of Armenians streamed into nearby Cilicia, where the long arm of the Seljuks had not yet reached. There, the

Rubenid dynasty founded the Armenian Principality of Cilicia in circa 1080. They might have been far from their ancestral homes, but the people were still Armenians, and here they were free to practice their culture and faith in relative peace.

Soon, these Armenians attracted the attention of another key player in this part of history: Pope Urban II.

The Byzantine emperor during the 1090s, Alexios I, had been begging the pope for help against a common enemy of the Christian world. Inspired by the prestige that he would gain if he managed to summon a combined army of Christian forces in a Europe that was being torn apart by petty wars among small kings, Urban was more than happy to help, calling an army together to attack the Holy Land, which was then under the control of those same Seljuks who had captured Armenia. The First Crusade was launched in 1095, and thousands of European troops traveled from as far away as Great Britain, France, and Germany and headed toward the utterly alien lands of the Middle East. And this is where the Armenian Principality of Cilicia caught their attention. In a world almost entirely dominated by Turks and Arabs, the Armenians might have been robbed of their homeland, but they had two things that the Crusaders needed: the Christian faith and fast horses.

The Armenians had brought some of their famous horses with them from their home, and when the Crusaders came to Cilicia asking for help, they were more than ready to assist them in conquering their mutual enemies. This small principality—arguably the first important Armenian diaspora community—became instrumental in the early successes of the First Crusade.

Sadly, however, the Armenian Principality of Cilicia would not be the last diaspora community that was forced to leave their home and thrive in a different world. A dark time was coming for Armenia. And considering all that the country's people had already suffered, it is significant that what was coming later would be the darkest time of them all.

Chapter 10 – Conquered

As Greater Armenia continued to suffer under the subjugation of the Seljuk Turks, the Armenian Principality of Cilicia—brief though its heyday was—flourished all the more as Crusaders continued to stream through on their quest to liberate the Holy Land. In fact, the little principality was growing in such importance that it was about to become a kingdom, led by a man named Levon of the Rubenid dynasty.

Levon II (also known as Leo) was born a prince of Cilicia. Growing up, he was the heir apparent, the younger brother to its childless lord, Roupen (or Ruben) III. Politics were strained and difficult. The Byzantine Empire, in a stunning twist of affairs, had allied itself with one of the most legendary Muslim leaders of the Middle Ages— Saladin. This move enraged the Holy Roman Empire, which had grown from the wreckage of ancient Rome and was an avid participant in the Crusades, as they were closely linked with the papacy. Its leader was Frederick Barbarossa, a red-bearded larger-than-life legend of a man who would fight anyone, especially if they happened to be a Muslim. When Saladin took Jerusalem in 1187, enjoying his lack of opposition from Byzantine forces elsewhere, it was all the reason that Barbarossa needed to launch the Third Crusade.

As usual, Cilicia was instrumental in the Crusade, this time more than ever. The principality had grown in size and importance, thanks to Levon's adept management. His brother Roupen had been betrayed and imprisoned by a former ally, and he was so shaken by the experience that when Levon had come to his rescue, he handed over the ruling of his principality to his younger brother in 1187. It was only two years later, thanks to his alliance with Holy Roman Emperor Henry VI (who succeeded Barbarossa, who drowned while recklessly trying to cross a river in the Third Crusade) and Pope Constantine III, that Levon became a king and the Armenian Principality of Cilicia was raised to the status of the Kingdom of Armenian Cilicia in 1198. The Byzantine emperor had also attempted to make Levon king, but the two kingdoms were never able to settle their theological differences, and so, the Holy Roman Empire and the papacy beat the Byzantines to it.

During Levon's reign, the Kingdom of Armenian Cilicia reached its very apogee. His rule, ending in his death in 1219, was an era of hope and glory for a desperate people. It became larger than ever before, occupying much of what is now southern Turkey. While the Armenians back in their own homeland were being oppressed by the Seljuks, their culture was free to flourish, and their church to gain importance, in Cilicia. It was a foothold for the Armenian people, one without which their culture—and the Crusades —might have turned out very differently.

The fate of Armenia itself, however, would be very different during the Middle Ages. One Muslim power after another—each controlled by legendary military leaders whose skill and brutality made them as famous in their time as they are in ours—would overrun this unhappy kingdom. There was a brief respite during the 12th and 13th centuries as the Kingdom of Georgia rose up to overthrow the Seljuk Turks and take back Armenia for Christianity, but it was nothing more than a breather between blows. An even more legendary warrior than Saladin was about to march on Armenia, one whose impact on humankind was devastating: Genghis Khan.

* * * *

To the people of Europe and the Middle East, the world was smartly divided along one strong line: Muslims on one side, Christians on the other. There were wars within those powers, of course, but religiously and racially, there was a sense of "us" and "them," an undeniable divide that characterized the Middle Ages. Over the six hundred years since Muhammad had walked the earth, the Muslims had become a familiar, if intimidating, foe. They had effectively wiped Zoroastrianism off the face of the earth, and polytheism was a thing of the past for the most part, with paganism being buried alongside the old Greek and Roman gods. At least, so the people thought. Genghis Khan, like some ancient monster long buried in a black abyss, rose from out of nowhere to wreak havoc of a very ancient flavor on everything he touched.

Genghis Khan was born as Temüjin, and even his conception occurred under dark and frightening circumstances. His mother had just gotten married to a young man she probably loved when Temüjin's father, Yesükhei, kidnapped her on her way home from her wedding. He forced her into a marriage with him, and Temüjin was the product of their union.

By the time he was only sixteen years old, Temüjin's father had been poisoned, and Temüjin himself had been imprisoned for five years after murdering his older brother. It is not hard to see where the brutality of Genghis Khan came from. But with that brutality also came military and diplomatic brilliance. By the age of 27, Temüjin was made khan, or leader, of the Mongols; by 42, he had unified the scattered tribes of the region into the single powerful entity of Mongolia. And ten years after that, he devastated China, a land of around fifty million citizens, with an army only 100,000 strong.

Genghis Khan swept across the world before him like a tsunami: brutal, unstoppable, destroying all in its path. His soldiers were dark-haired, dark-eyed horsemen from a different world than the Middle Eastern people that he attacked once most of Central Asia was within his far-reaching grasp. It was not long before he turned to Armenia. To him, it was nothing, just a little kingdom, one more small jewel in his treasury. But to the people his forces would butcher, it was home.

Armenia, at the time, was a divided kingdom, split up between the powers that continued to war over it. Northern and Eastern Armenia belonged to the Georgian kingdoms, ruled by a branch of the Bagratid family, the same family that had once elevated medieval Armenia to greatness. In the west, the Seljuks still maintained their grasp on the kingdom. And in a handful of small provinces in the south, ethnic Armenians had managed to claw back some semblance of independence for their little group of people. But all that would change between around 1220 and 1240 when the Mongols decided that Armenia would be theirs.

The Mongol conquest of Armenia, however, did not take place with the steamroller efficiency that many other hapless countries had experienced when they fell to the wrath of the Mongols. It took twenty years and almost as much diplomatic negotiating as warfare; each move on the part of the Mongols was a carefully calculated strategic maneuver, brilliantly executed. The invasion of Armenia, which finally fell around 1240, was more proof than ever that Genghis Khan—for all his brutality—was more than just a terrorizing force of evil. He was a military genius, lauded in the East as much as he was feared and hated in the West.

* * * *

As Armenia was held in the icy grip of the Mongol hordes, the Kingdom of Armenian Cilicia continued to thrive on the Crusade-rich environment of the 13th century, so much so that it was soon no longer known as Cilicia. Instead, it was so densely populated by Armenians that it was given a new name: Lesser Armenia.

The Rubenid dynasty had intermarried with and been absorbed into the Hethumid dynasty in Lesser Armenia, and when the Mongols swept across Greater Armenia and captured much of Asia Minor, the king of Lesser Armenia, Hethum I, knew that his country would suffer the same fate if it dared to defy the Mongols. Instead, he formed an alliance with them, an act that may feel treacherous in retrospect but one that saved his country from being overrun the way Greater Armenia was. Hethum and his men fought in the Mongolian campaigns that continued across the Middle East.

But the Mongols were not as invincible as they appeared. Their campaigns would grind to a halt in the face of a class of warrior slaves whose loyalties lay with no one: the Mamluks.

An important part of Muslim armies, the Mamluks were property, but they were extremely valuable. Taken from their families as young boys, they were raised in the barracks, giving them no one to be loyal to except their owners and one another. Raised and trained for war and nothing else, the Mamluks fought with a professional kind of dedication, as their whole lives were devoted to battle. The Egyptian Mamluks were among the only soldiers who ever successfully stood against the Mongols, and they did so in the mid-13th century, drawing a firm eastern border of the Mongolian conquest. Even Genghis Khan did not get past them.

This had devastating consequences for Lesser Armenia, which was a powerful rival to the Muslim world, thanks to its control of the spice trade and also its support of the Crusades. The Mamluk leader demanded that Hethum switch his alliance from Mongolia to Egypt. Knowing that he was facing a tremendous foe, Hethum fled to the Mongol court to beg for help. In his absence, the Mamluks invaded Lesser Armenia and conquered it, all but destroying the country in 1266.

An earthquake shattered whatever the Mamluks had left standing just two years later. And while it would cling to its status as a kingdom for a little over another century, albeit a shadow of its former self and constantly harried by the Muslim forces, Lesser Armenia's days were numbered. The Turkic and Mamluk armies eventually tore it up into pieces, and by the Mamluk invasion of 1375, Lesser Armenia was a kingdom no more. Its Armenian inhabitants fled to Cyprus, France, and other countries. The home that had sheltered them for hundreds of years was gone.

* * * *

In its long history, Armenia had faced many devastating conquerors. It had been trampled and torn down by ancient Rome, by Alexander the Great, and even by Genghis Khan. But one of the most dreaded—and the most legendary—men ever to claim Armenia's highlands as his own was Timur the Lame, better known in the West as Tamerlane.

During the 14th century, the spectacular power of the Mongols began to fade in the wake of Genghis Khan's death. Armenia might have been free, but the Mongols were briskly supplanted by a Turkic nation, the Chupanids, also spelled as the Chobanids.

Armenia had not been an independent kingdom since the time of the Bagratuni family. Even Lesser Armenia was gone now; the heart of the Armenian people was as oppressed as their physical bodies. Generations of Armenians did not know what it meant to be free, and they would not be free again for another five hundred years. The next conqueror who rose up against them was Tamerlane, and he devastated Armenia in a way that even this much-defeated people had never experienced before. For it was by the hand of Tamerlane that the first Turkish massacre of the Armenians was performed.

By the time he invaded Armenia and Georgia, Tamerlane had become a legend, a bogeyman that was all too real. Born in modern Uzbekistan, Tamerlane was a nobody, and a disabled one at that, as a childhood injury left his right side crippled. He grew up as a kind of amateur highwayman, mugging innocent travelers with his friends, despite the fact that his father was a wealthy minor noble, and his desire to conquer did not end there. By the year 1400, Tamerlane had beaten the messy tribes of his area into an unstoppable army, unifying a scattered region in much the same way as Genghis Khan had done. He had defeated both Persia and India, and he had proven himself more powerful even than the Mamluks. So, Armenia was no match for him. Tamerlane did not just invade the country: he utterly destroyed it. Witnesses described how he would destroy a thousand-year-old city in a single day, his forces even going so far as to dig up ancient fortifications, and his scorched-earth policy left nothing untouched. Nothing left alive.

As for the people, they suffered under Tamerlane as they had never suffered before. Men, women, children, Christians, pagans—it didn't matter to him. He just wanted them dead, all of them. The accounts of Tamerlane's massacre are absolutely chilling, as they describe how he had Armenians thrown from the city walls to their deaths in such numbers that the piles of corpses grew and grew to the extent that their dead bodies cushioned some of the last victims. It is difficult to comprehend the terror that those last victims must have experienced; lying there, their limbs broken, their skin crushed, upon a great pile of their fellow citizens, as they died slowly and tangled amid the corpses of their own countrymen.

What Tamerlane did to the Armenians was brutal. But it was just a taste, a brief foreshadowing of what was coming.

Chapter 11 – The First Deportation

One of the races that Tamerlane would face in his bid to defeat the whole of Asia and Europe was also Turkic like him: the Ottomans. And long after Tamerlane's Timurid Empire had melted away into history, the Ottoman Turks would continue to build an empire that would last for centuries.

The Timurid Empire, founded by Tamerlane, effectively ended Mongol power. It controlled a vast stretch of Europe and Asia, including modern-day Iran, Afghanistan, Turkmenistan, Uzbekistan, Tajikistan, Iraq, India, Pakistan, Syria, and Armenia. Tamerlane's capital, Samarkand, was known as the "Center of the World," and it was here that Tamerlane proved himself to be a dedicated patron of the arts and culture—which is ironic considering how badly he had devastated Armenian culture. His conquests killed almost twenty million people, but his empire would not last for long. Like Alexander's, it was divided up after his death. By the beginning of the 16th century, the Timurid Empire was no more, although one of its branches, the Mughal Empire, would last in India until the mid-19th century.

With the Mongols and the Timurids gone, and the Holy Roman Empire already starting to lose power and crumble under its own weight, there was a vacuum of power in the Middle East and Asia Minor. That vacuum would be filled by a Turkish superpower that had already started making its presence felt in the time of Tamerlane.

The Ottoman Turks were born on the very doorstep of Armenia. Originating in the mountains of Anatolia, the Ottomans were little more than just another Turkish tribe, much like the Chupanids, who had lost their grip on Armenia by now; Armenia had become a battleground once again between rivaling tribes until the time of Mehmed II. Known as Mehmed the Conqueror, he transformed the Ottomans into more than just some little tribe. They became a nation and, later, an empire. Like most Turks, Mehmed and his people were Muslims. It was a crushing blow for all of Christianity—and an enormous triumph for the Islamic world—when Mehmed defeated Byzantium, now Constantinople. The ancient Byzantine Empire had already been weakened, and Mehmed's attack in 1453 was the nail in the coffin. He made Constantinople his own capital, and so, the Ottoman Empire was born.

Of course, for the hapless Armenians, this was not good. Mehmed conquered Cilicia and imprisoned the Armenian population that still lived there, which mostly consisted of lower-class people who had not been able to flee when it was first invaded by the Mamluks in the late 14th century. Mehmed moved many of them to Constantinople, where conditions proved to be so unbearable that thousands of Armenians undertook a migration to Bruges, Belgium. A diaspora community 30,000 strong thrives there to this day.

The Ottoman Empire continued to grow, especially during the rule of Suleiman the Magnificent. It reached its height in the 16th century, absorbing Syria, Egypt, Palestine, Bulgaria, Romania, Jordan, Lebanon, parts of Arabia and Africa, Hungary, and Greece, among others.

Yet even with the Byzantine, Timurid, and Mongol Empires out of the way, the Ottomans did not find themselves wholly unopposed as they entered the 16th and 17th centuries. Persia, which was devastated by Arabia in the 7th century, was about to rise again one more time. And this time, it would be more glorious than ever.

Claiming to be descendants of Tamerlane, the Safavid dynasty of Persia rose to power in 1501. Their rule would continue until the 18th century, ushering in the Golden Age of Persia and bringing Persia onto a collision course with the Ottoman Empire.

The Sasanid Persians had been Zoroastrians, but centuries of Arabic rule had converted Persia to Islam. Even since the days just after Muhammad, however, Islam itself had been divided into two sects: the Sunni Muslims and the Shi'ite Muslims. The Ottomans were Sunnis, as most Muslims are today. But the Persians were Shi'ites, and that made them worse than infidels in the eyes of the Ottomans. To make matters worse, the Safavids wanted to expand Persia once again into the mighty empire that it once had been, and the Ottomans were in the way. And, once again, Armenia would find itself caught in the crossfire.

The Ottoman-Persian Wars would rage for more than three hundred years, and in that time, Armenia would be beaten back and forth like a ping-pong ball between two players who cared nothing for the ball; they only cared about winning the game. For everyday Armenians, this was everything but a game. Life was a battleground, and no city was safe from one horde or the other that came trampling across the mountainside without regard for the people whose lives were being constantly uprooted, changed, or, routinely, ended. Yerevan itself, now the capital of Armenia, was passed back and forth seventeen times over the course of the wars.

To make matters worse, the Jelālī Revolts, a series of clashes once again between Sunni and Shi'ite Muslims, took place in Armenia and Anatolia around this time. Yet even with warring soldiers of all kinds of other faiths around them, the Armenians managed to cling to one aspect of their national identity: their faith. They remained staunchly Christian, even though this made both the Ottomans and the Persians treat them as somehow inferior. One example of how poorly the Ottomans treated Armenians was with something called the devshirme system, aptly nicknamed "blood tax." In this tax, boys from Christian villages in Armenia and its surroundings were kidnapped by the state, forcibly converted to Islam, and then made to serve the government for the rest of their lives.

Yet it was not the Ottomans who would subject Armenians to the greatest cruelty they suffered in the 16th century. It was the Persians.

* * * *

The Araxes River was swollen and hot and angry, water plunging between its banks like a wild animal bent on breaking its bonds. Its foaming waters roared even louder than the thunder of thousands of hooves and hundreds of thousands of feet, louder even than the crack of the cannons in the distance as 300,000 Armenian villagers tramped warily up to the bursting banks. The same river that had given the ancient Kura-Araxes people their name was now earning its own name of "fast-flowing." The waters were swift and deadly, and even knowing that there was an Ottoman horde on their heels, the villagers ground to a halt. They looked up at the soldiers accompanying them, unbelieving. On either side of the river, the wreckage of what had once been a bridge was barely visible. How were they supposed to get across the river?

Shah Abbās I the Great, the king of Safavid Persia, had not counted on having to flee back this way when he had ordered his armies to destroy the bridge behind them. He was a gifted military leader, a commander who had led his army to victory after victory against the Ottomans. He had believed that laying siege to Kars, an Armenian city, in 1604 would be just another victory. Only it wasn't. Abbas had no choice but to retreat, and his hard struggle against the Ottomans had taught him an even harder lesson: the only way to beat them was to leave them with nothing. He had to destroy every village that he left behind in order to avoid allowing the Ottomans to find resources in the rich highlands of Armenia.

Abbās' men had butchered the Armenians' animals. They had burned their homes and razed their villages and towns to the very ground, then burned the grass so that there was nothing left. They had told the Armenians that it was for their own good. They had told the Armenians to come with them for their own safety, to avoid being murdered by the Ottomans, and for a time, the Armenians had trusted them. The Persians were Muslims, but on the whole, Abbās had been tolerant of his Christian subjects so far.

But now, the king was desperate. He knew the Ottomans were in hot pursuit, and 300,000 milling villagers had slowed him down. Knowing that his fit soldiers on their strong horses would ford the river easily, Abbās ordered them to cross.

The Armenians knew they could not make it. Clutching their children close, they watched him with wide eyes. One of them— brave or foolish or perhaps just fed up and exhausted after what had already been a long march—tried to break ranks and flee back to what was left of his home. A gunshot rang out, and the man dropped dead in a pool of blood.

Trapped between the murderous Persians and the deadly river, the Armenians had no choice. They had to take their chances with the water—and those chances were slim. Old people and young children and the sick and simply those caught off guard by the icy, rushing waters found themselves overwhelmed in seconds. Soon, corpses were flowing through the river like flood debris, bumping against the living as they attempted to cross the raging water. Thousands of them perished in the Araxes that day, and it was just the beginning of what was to come.

During the long march through the middle of winter to the safety of Isfahan, a city in Persia, the Armenian villagers perished in the hundreds of thousands. Those who resisted the march were swiftly and brutally dispatched by the soldiers; those who did not die realized that no provisions had been made to feed them. The sound of thousands of crying children filled the air, following the marchers wherever they went like a clinging cloud of black mist. They died like flies, leaving behind a trail of withered, skeletal corpses. Those most desperate picked at those corpses, feeding on the human flesh in a bid to simply survive.

By the time the march was over, less than 150,000 of those villagers remained alive. Even though Abbās had not directly attacked the Armenians as a people, he had wrought the same atrocities on them as Tamerlane and Genghis Khan.

The Safavids had not treated the Armenians well, but like many empires that had come and gone before them, they would not last forever. Albeit clinging on to Eastern Armenia for another two hundred years, the Safavid Empire began to decline in the 18th century as both the Ottomans and Russia fought against it. By 1828, Armenia was once again divided among two conquering kingdoms: Western Armenia belonging to the Muslim Ottomans and Eastern Armenia to the Christian Russians. The Safavid Empire was no more, having collapsed in 1736.

The majority of ethnic Armenians were now living in the vast and bloated Ottoman Empire as the 19th century wore on. Suffice it to say that the Ottomans did not treat them well. As religious freedom became more of a theme across the globe, the Ottomans continued to use the millet system—a way of dividing people along racial and religious lines and taxing them accordingly. Armenians, who still clung constantly to Christianity, were considered to be some of the most inferior people in the empire. They were taxed far more heavily than their Muslim counterparts. Somehow, though, the Armenians managed to thrive within the empire, their numbers reaching an all-time high. They were used to oppression; they had endured it for generations, and they knew how to survive—and even how to succeed—without the freedoms that so much of the world took for granted.

The Ottomans had taken their children. The Persians had taken their lives. But what Armenia had suffered was nothing in comparison to what was coming next. They would be the first nation to endure the greatest crime of all: genocide.

Chapter 12 – Genocide

Illustration IV: Hapless Armenians undertake a forced march

The screams of the young woman in labor echoed across the desert. They were ripping sounds, holding so much more than the primal agony of childbirth. They shredded the air with a razor-sharp terror, bursting with loneliness, with desperation. The young girl walking beside the horse had heard women in labor before in the rural village that had once been her world, a village that felt like it was a thousand years away now. It sounded painful, but it also sounded like something of hope, as if even in that agony, an expectant mother knew that a new life was being brought forth. But the girl's sister screamed in simple pain. There was no hope in her voice. There was no hope in the barren landscape through which the long ribbon of desolate marchers moved. There was no hope in their empty eyes as they gazed down at the ground at their feet, avoiding the bloodstains and the corpses and the places where others had squatted down to relieve themselves, having nowhere else to go. There was no hope in the way they walked with their slumped shoulders, not even looking up as the woman's shrieks continued to reverberate from dune to dune across the Syrian Desert. There was not even interest because her screams were not the only ones to resound through this hopeless wilderness. Here, a child was crying, begging for food; there, a baby moaning in one steady monotone, as it had been doing for days, as it would not do for much longer; and not far away, a girl was being raped, a man butchered with a blade, a mother crumbling down in grief by the side of her child.

There were worse reasons to scream than childbirth. But could there be a worse childbirth than this young mother was enduring? The soldiers had refused to let her stop. One, kinder than the others (the others might simply have butchered her), had lifted her onto his horse. And now, on that moving animal, she was bringing a baby girl out into the world.

A world that hated them. A world that had rejected them.

* * * *

This eyewitness account was told in abrupt and simple terms by a young girl who was only twelve years old when she was ripped from her home. She was lucky enough to survive the genocide, but around one million Armenians were not so lucky.

By the late 19th century, Armenia had endured more than can really be believed. The fact that the Armenians still had a national and cultural identity—one that was stronger than ever as the Christian Armenian communities lived a life so separate from their Turkish neighbors—is almost surprising, considering what they had been through so far. Yet the darkest period in Armenian history was yet to come. The genocide would soon begin.

The first taste of this level of destruction occurred in 1894. The Ottoman Empire was in decline, and its sultan, Abdul Hamid II, was well aware of this fact. An exceptionally paranoid and corrupt ruler, Abdul Hamid feared nothing more than losing parts of the empire, and the fact that it was crumbling at the edges terrified him. Instead of working to unite the empire, however, he struck out at an ethnic minority that posed little threat to him: the Armenians. Although the Armenian Revolutionary Federation (ARF) had caused some rebellions in parts of the country, most of the Armenian people were fairly peace-loving, as no doubt were many of the Muslim Turks. But Abdul Hamid continued to tell all who would listen that the Armenians were dangerous, that they were going to be the downfall of the empire. His brainwashing inevitably began to take effect, and the Turks began to regard their Armenian neighbors with growing suspicion.

Things came to a head in the Susan region when taxes were raised and a small group of Armenians refused to pay up. There is no record that these people were at all violent, but Abdul Hamid's men did not need to see any violence to strike first. Tensions erupted, and soldiers opened fire on the civilian Armenians. It was only the first of several waves of killings between 1894 and 1896, with Turkish soldiers and even some civilians turning against the Armenians. Carrying weapons was illegal if you were Armenian; these people were defenseless, and they were slaughtered like cattle. Around

300,000 Armenians died during this time, in what is called the Hamidian massacres.

With eerie and appalling familiarity, another spate of killings erupted in 1909. By then, the Young Turks—a progressive group of revolutionaries with visions for a more modern and diplomatic Ottoman Empire—had risen up to overthrow Abdul Hamid and take hold of the government in 1908. The Young Turk Revolution was a day so joyous that Muslims and Christians had embraced each other on the streets, a day where Armenians and Turks stood side by side with the hope of equality at last. That hope was dimmed in April 1909. Supporters of Abdul Hamid staged a revolt, and instead of fighting the Turks, they fought the Armenians, who could not fight back. In the city of Adana, part of what had once been the Armenian Kingdom of Cilicia, 30,000 Armenians were ruthlessly murdered. American missionaries, for their part, suffered alongside them.

But the Adana and Hamidian massacres, devastating though they were, were nothing compared to the genocide proper.

When the Young Turks regained control over the empire after the Adana massacre, there was a vague hope that perhaps things would be better with them in charge. It was a useless, misplaced hope. Instead of working toward the unity of a diverse empire, the Young Turks—now the leaders of the Committee of Union and Progress, or CUP, the leading political party of the Ottomans—decided that there was only one way to present a united front to a world on the brink of World War I. This was "Turkification": the presentation of Turkish identity that was seen as being utterly vital to the survival of the empire. Accordingly, anyone who was not Turkish—anyone who was, for example, Armenian—was nothing short of a direct threat to the Ottoman Empire's survival.

While the Turkification campaign proved disastrous for religious and ethnic minorities, the Young Turks' fear, albeit misplaced, was understandable. Tensions across the globe had never been higher, and for a failing empire, a world war could spell disaster. But a world war was coming. In desperate need of a strong ally, when the First World War erupted in 1914, the Ottomans entered in it on the side of their allies, Germany and the Austro-Hungarian Empire. Less understandable was the Ottomans' next decision: to declare war not only on Germany's enemies but also on all Christians excepting the Germans. For the Ottomans, the "Great War" was even more than a world war. It was a holy one.

Considering there had been practically no repercussions for the perpetrators of the Adana and Hamidian massacres, it is unsurprising that the Armenians quickly became the perceived public enemy of the Ottoman Empire. Having weathered rebellions in the Balkans, and having lost the Balkan Wars with devastating consequences for the empire, the Ottoman soldiers viewed the Armenians as being potentially dangerous. But their government blew this suspicion way out of proportion. With the Ottoman borders under attack, the Turks turned their attention instead to their own population, electing to eradicate an entire race.

The Armenian Genocide began on April 24th, 1915, when hundreds of Armenian intellectuals were arrested, imprisoned, and, later, deported. These were middle- to upper-class people who contributed to Ottoman society as scientists, artists, writers, and thinkers; it is probable that all of them were innocent of any kind of rebellion. Yet they soon found themselves on a forced march across the Syrian Desert, to be expelled from the bowels of the empire and vomited up like something poisonous even though they posed no threat.

Over the next seven years, hundreds of thousands of Armenians would be expelled from their homes, and the cruelty did not end with deportation. These people were butchered. Even helpless orphans were ordered to be killed as the Ottoman treatment of the Armenians quickly blossomed into a full-blown attempt to exterminate the entire race once and for all. As persecuted as the Armenians had been for centuries, they had never suffered like this.

They were killed by the thousands in almost every way imaginable. Shot on the death marches across the desert. Gutted with swords in gruesome ways in order to frighten those who yet survived. Starved. Beaten. Raped. In one awful instance, five thousand were gathered together, tied to a pile of dry grass, and burned to death, their shrieks echoing across the homeland where their people had lived for untold thousands of years. The children were inoculated with blood that was infected with typhus; the people were overdosed on morphine, gassed, or herded onto ships and then thrown overboard within sight of the city of Trebizond. Thousands of children were sold off as slaves—sometimes sex slaves—to Muslim households. And while many Muslim civilians did their part in a bid to save the Armenians (with some accounts telling of Muslim men marrying whole groups of Armenian women to save them from certain death), some turned on their own neighbors as they had done in the Hamidian and Adana massacres and butchered them in the streets.

By 1922, the Armenian population had been utterly decimated. There had been around 1.5 million Armenians in the empire prior to 1915. When the genocide finally ended as World War I came to a close and the world woke up to the reality of what had taken place, there were only 388,000 left. About three-quarters of the Armenian population was dead. For every person left alive, three were gone. For every family of four, only one was left. Those who had lived were all grieving the loss of three-quarters of the people they knew, and a terrible, gaping wound was left where those people once had been, as Muslim families moved into the homes from which the Armenians had been so forcefully wrested.

The Armenian Genocide was a chapter of history that cannot, and will not, be forgotten —despite the best efforts of even the modern Turkish government. Even to this very day, Turkey refuses to admit that what occurred was truly genocide, even though experts in this grave field widely accept that the events of 1915 to 1922 were genocide. In fact, it is illegal in Turkey to even mention what was done to the Armenians, and to this day, many countries—including the US—do not officially recognize the genocide. The Holocaust is common knowledge; the Armenian Genocide is obscure history, in part thanks to Turkey's denial of its historical sins.

Chapter 13 – Freedom at Last

General Drastamat Kanayan, "Dro" to friends and to history, had wanted to be a soldier ever since he was a little boy. As a kid, he would play hooky to watch the Russian soldiers at the barracks near his home. Their drills and exercises fascinated him, and as yet another Armenian child living under the control of a foreign empire, perhaps something about their force and control appealed to his young heart. At least Russian Armenians were not persecuted for their religion as they were in the Ottoman Empire, but they were still a long way from being free.

Yet fighting alongside them still seemed better than living the ordinary life that Dro's time at school was leading him toward. Noticing that his son was hopeless in school, Dro's father sent him to the military school in Yerevan. The boy's grades barely improved, but his love for all things military grew nothing short of insatiable. It was a logical next step to become a soldier after graduation. It was all he had ever wanted to do.

And he had never truly desired to be a Russian soldier. He wanted to be an Armenian one, so much so that he secretly joined an underground youth movement opposing Russian rule. Nothing ever came of the movement, but it inspired Dro's heart, and in all the years since—years spent fighting the First World War on the Russian side—he had not let go of that inspiration.

Yet today, now, as he looked out over the battlefield thrown wide before him, Dro was not so sure that he really was cut out for the role in which history had cast him. He had wanted to fight for his people ever since he was a kid, but perhaps he had not realized how high the stakes could become. On the outskirts of Sardarapat, less than twenty miles from his home in Yerevan, Dro was watching the advance of an army that he knew his forces could not hope to beat. Ten thousand Ottomans. Three thousand Kurdish cavalry, legendary for their outrageous bloodthirst. Forty great cannons, and at any moment, their devastating crack would ring out across the mountains and rain death upon the group of Armenians at Dro's side. There were 9,000 of them; they were not as badly outnumbered as they could have been, but the Ottomans were trained soldiers, veterans of four years of the world war. And the Armenians...Dro scanned his ranks, letting out a little sigh. There were a handful of real soldiers, of course, but most of the people standing by his side were nobodies. Blacksmiths and butchers. Farmers and grocers. They were armed with whatever he and his men were able to rustle up on such short notice. How could they hope to stand against the Ottomans?

He looked further back, beyond the ranks of his men, toward the roads leading to Yerevan, and they were black with carts and people. Water buffalo and donkeys and even the sagging old shapes of skinny dairy cows were harnessed to those carts, women and little children driving the beasts up to the army, and the carts were piled high with everything that they could get their hands on: food, water, medical supplies, crude weaponry. Dro's heart flipped over in his chest. This was the Armenian people. They were all standing with him, behind him, watching a purely Armenian army go out to battle for its own people for the first time in centuries. The people were looking up at him like he was Tigranes the Great, or Hayk, or some hero. Some hero who could rebuild the glory days of Urartu and the Armenian Empire.

Dro raised his chin and watched the Ottomans coming, and he knew that the odds were slim. But he also knew that he had to try. No one was coming to rescue Armenia.

It was time for them to rescue themselves.

* * * *

As the genocide raged in the Ottoman Empire, there was only one region of historic Armenia that could still be considered safe: the tiny slice of Eastern Armenia that had remained under the control of the Russian Empire. Albeit a small portion of the once-mighty country, Eastern Armenia was the very heart of the ancient land, containing Mount Ararat and the once-capital, Yerevan. It was still considered a Russian protectorate, and with the tremendous power of the Russian army defending it, it was the one place where the Armenians could go and the Ottomans could not follow.

Refugees streamed into Eastern Armenia as the genocide continued unabated. The Russians had seized Armenian Church property and made lives difficult for their Armenian subjects, but at least they had not murdered a million of them. Anything would be better than the Ottomans.

But at the eleventh hour, shortly after the Bolsheviks seized power in Moscow, Russia pulled out. The Russian troops that had been guarding hundreds of thousands of refugees in Eastern Armenia simply packed up and headed back home upon Bolshevik orders, leaving the Armenians utterly defenseless against the invading masses of the Ottoman army. It was May 1918; World War I had all but destroyed Europe, and each country was scrambling wildly to hold on to its own freedom. No one was coming to save the Armenians. What was left of them, at least.

If the Battle of Sardarapat, which took place in late May 1918, had turned out differently, there would be no Armenia on the map today.

In fact, the very Armenian race may have been as wholly exterminated as the Ottomans had hoped. The vast majority of the surviving Armenian population was living in Eastern Armenia, and if the Ottomans overran it, they would no doubt subject them to the same treatment as their Western cousin. Dro and his men were not just fighting for independence—they were fighting for the very survival of their own race. The stakes had never been higher.

But May 28th, 1918, would go down in history as the day that Armenia was set free once again. Because that was the day that the ragged Armenian army, composed mostly of volunteers, drew a line in the sand and said, "This far and no farther." That was the day that the borders of modern Armenia were drawn, the day that the Armenian people were saved not by the Romans or the Byzantine Empire or the Mongols but by themselves, their own people, depleted of their resources, stripped of their pride, their identity trampled, their race decimated, their allies vanished. They had nothing except the burning courage that had kept them clinging on to their faith, to their culture, to who they were. They had nothing but their identity, and on that day, their identity was enough. Armenia was forced to stand for itself. And stand it did.

The Battle of Sardarapat was Armenia's rebirth, a baptism in blood, as Dro and the rest of the generals and barefoot volunteers that surrounded him held back the Ottomans on the banks of the Araxes, the selfsame river where the Persians had drowned thousands of Armenians on the eve of the very first mass killing in the 17th century. But not today. Today the Ottomans fell in untold numbers, and the Armenians fought back, and they won.

The Ottoman Empire was forced into a disorganized retreat, their armies fleeing back into their own lands. Eastern Armenia would never see Turkish rule again. And while the genocide would continue in Western Armenia for another four years, those who managed to flee to the mountains around Yerevan were saved. The Armenian race would live on, not so much surviving as being resurrected in the blazing light of Sardarapat.

* * * *

May 28th, 1918, became the date commemorated for the founding of the First Republic of Armenia. Dro was its defense minister; his fellow general, Tovmas Nazarbekian, became the commander-in-chief. It was the first time in centuries that Armenia would be independent, even if it was just a tiny slice of Armenia for now.

This independence would be short-lived, but it was incredible while it lasted. The Ottoman Empire and its allies ended World War I in defeat, and it was the nail in the coffin for the declining empire. Its territories were granted independence or divided among the conquering nations; the Republic of Armenia was one of those who became independent, and on October 30th, 1918, it was able to annex Western Armenia as well. The ancient nation was whole once more. And in 1922, the Ottoman Empire finally breathed its last, reemerging as the Republic of Turkey in 1923. It was only when the Ottoman Empire ended that the genocide stopped, too.

For two years, the Republic of Armenia started to try and piece together a decimated country. How do you rebuild a nation with three-quarters of its population dead? Courageous volunteers, some from across the globe, began to work to rescue the women and children that had been kidnapped and enslaved during the genocide, and slowly, the Republic of Armenia began to take form. Sadly, it would not last for long.

The Bolsheviks that had so easily abandoned Armenia to its fate were suddenly becoming interested in the nation once more, now that it was so much larger and proving that it was still worth something, despite the devastation that it had suffered. The Armenian Soviet Socialist Republic was established as a political organization in December 1920, and it opposed the Republic of Armenia, alongside the Russians and Turkey. With grisly déjà vu, Armenia was caught in the crossfire of Turkey and the Soviet Union, just like it had been so many times during its history. The First Republic of Armenia couldn't hope to stand against the USSR-backed Armenian Soviet Socialist Republic. The Russians took the east, the Turks took the west, and Eastern Armenia became a part of the Soviet Union in 1923. As for Western Armenia, it remains a part of Turkey to this day, and barely a handful of ethnic Armenians still live there. The genocide was successful in removing the Armenian question from Western Armenia entirely.

Life in Armenia under the Soviet Union became rapidly unbearable. The Turks had belittled and looked down on Armenians for their faith, and the Russians arrested them for it. Joseph Stalin's bid to eradicate religion entirely within the Soviet Union was an unspeakable cruelty to many Armenians, for whom their beloved faith was the only thing they had left after surviving the genocide. To some among them, taking away Christianity may have felt like an even worse crime than genocide itself. The faith still survived, however, as Christians met in secret to hide the fact that they still worshiped in defiance of Stalin.

Muslim Armenians, of whom there were by this time a significant number, were not exempt from this cruelty, either. They suffered right alongside their Christian counterparts; thousands of them were deported from Georgia to Uzbekistan in 1944.

But like all of the empires that had controlled Armenia, the Soviet Union would not last forever. Despite emerging from World War II more powerful than ever before, and becoming a looming threat to the capitalist world during the long era of tensions known as the Cold War, the Soviet Union began to decline in the late 20th century. By 1991, the Berlin Wall came crashing down, and the Soviet Union died just like all of those old empires that had tried to make Armenia theirs.

The Romans, the Byzantines, the Mongols, the Arabs, the Parthians, the Persians, the Timurids, the Ottomans, the Soviets—they had all been powerful once, and they had all faded out of Armenia's history. But this tiny country, having suffered so much, having endured more than can be imagined, was still holding on. And for the first time in many, many years, it was free.

Chapter 14 – A Study in Velvet

Illustration V: A snow-capped Mount Ararat in the distance

Serzh Sargsyan was nervous, a strange fact considering that he had been involved in politics since he was just a twenty-something in the 70s. Now a hawk-eyed man with an imposing presence and a crop of snow-white hair, Sargsyan walked into the meeting room on April 22nd, 2018, with an attempt at haughtiness. He had been the prime minister of Armenia, had been the president for ten years, and had just been elected as prime minister once again. Surely, of all the people of Armenia, Sargsyan had nothing to fear. Yet there was something in his darting dark eyes, in the way he smoothed down his shiny gray suit, that suggested that the pride in his bearing hid a note of fear.

It would have been deeply strange for Sargsyan to feel fear here and now. The room was large and empty except for a significant gaggle of camera-toting journalists, a cluster of microphones, and a slightly chubby middle-aged man in a camo T-shirt and an Adidas ball cap sitting on a chair by the microphones. This man, Nikol Pashinyan, a political nobody (except for the fact that he had been imprisoned for his rebellious writings) and the head of a minuscule political party named the Civil Contract, was himself looking a little wary. He fiddled with the straps of his rucksack as Sargsyan took his place across from him.

Sargsyan regarded Pashinyan for a moment, then spoke in a falsely jovial tone. He thanked Pashinyan for finally agreeing to meet with him after several days of attempting to make contact. Pashinyan's eyes were everywhere except on Sargsyan, perhaps a little overwhelmed. He had started his quiet walk from his home in Gyumri a little over three weeks earlier. Since then, pacing through the streets of Armenia, he had made his way to Yerevan. He was worn and travel-stained and tired, but he had succeeded in his objective: an audience with the prime minister, whose election had sparked Pashinyan's peaceful march. He had only agreed to speak to Sargsyan regarding his resignation as prime minister, but it would soon be clear that Sargsyan had no intentions to do so.

Having thanked Pashinyan for his presence, Sargsyan turned to the journalists and gave them a wide, white smile. He told Pashinyan cheerfully that he was not sure how to negotiate in front of so many people—a move that hinted at the ten years of corruption that had characterized his time as commander-in-chief of Armenia.

Pashinyan's face was still nervous, but his voice was calm and steady when he spoke up. "I came here to discuss the conditions of your resignation."

Sargsyan scoffed. He told Pashinyan that made their conversation something different from a resignation—it made it blackmail. "You did not learn the lesson of March 1st," he stated furiously.

Pashinyan looked up then, and his eyes flashed. March 1st, 2008. The day of Sargsyan's election as president, and the day that protests erupted all across Yerevan as the public made it clear that they knew the election had been rigged. Ten people had died when the police had opened fire on the protesters. Pashinyan had been there; he had been arrested for being there and had become a political prisoner for years. He knew that Sargsyan's words were a thinly veiled threat to the hundreds of peaceful protesters across Yerevan now, all on strike in a bid to support Pashinyan.

"The whole responsibility is on you," Sargsyan told the younger man, a bid to make him a scapegoat for the bloodbath that he was determined to make this protest into. "Choose."

Pashinyan's voice did not rise. "Nobody can talk with us in the language of threats," he said calmly. "The power in the Republic of Armenia transferred to the people."

At that, Sargsyan laughed out loud. "The group which got seven or eight percent in the election has not the right to talk in the name of a nation," he said sharply.

It was true that Pashinyan's party had been barely a blip on the radar in the recent elections, but Pashinyan knew that the world was changing. As Sargsyan ranted about how he did not want to continue the conversation, Pashinyan cast his eyes to the floor. "Goodbye," he said. Then, sharper, "Goodbye!"

Sargsyan gave him a last angry glare. He launched to his feet and strode from the room, leaving Pashinyan to address the journalists with a quiet confidence. A confidence that was not misplaced. In just a few weeks, Pashinyan's words would be proven true. And not a single shot would be fired.

The truth was that Pashinyan was right. March 1st, 2008, had seen an Armenia still wet behind the ears from the birth of its independence. Its military and police force had fired on the protesting crowds on Sargsyan's order, not questioning his authority. But the ten years that passed had begun to remind the Armenians that they could be more than this. They *would* be more than this. As the protest—always utterly peaceful—gathered strength, Sargsyan became more and more nervous. But the protesters never turned violent. There was no looting; Pashinyan had commanded as much. There was no chaos. And at ten every evening, the protesters all went home, only to return fresh-faced the next morning and peacefully voice the fact that they were done with corruption.

When Sargsyan demanded that the police should stop them, he realized the extent of Pashinyan's revolution because none of the officers would listen to him anymore. The corrupt leader had no one left to follow him, and he knew he was beaten. By May 8th, Nikol Pashinyan, the nobody, had become the president of Armenia. His protests became known as the Velvet Revolution for their gentleness.

* * * *

The Republic of Armenia had been plagued by corruption ever since its first election on October 17th, 1991. But in the early days of the republic, there were much bigger issues to deal with, and the Nagorno-Karabakh War was chief among them.

The Nagorno-Karabakh War started back in the time of Stalin when swathes of ancient Armenia were given to modern-day Azerbaijan instead of to the ethnic Armenians living in Eastern Armenia. This immediately sparked discontent in Armenia, especially considering that tempers were still simmering about the genocide, as the Azerbaijani populating the region were a Turkic people that bore many similarities to the Ottoman Turks who had brought so much grief to the Armenians. At first, the powerful Soviet Union was able to keep Azerbaijan and Armenia from actually coming to blows over the issue—neither of the smaller countries was willing to get on the USSR's nerves too much. But as the Soviet Union's power began to decline in the 1980s, the enclave of Nagorno-Karabakh became the topic of heated arguments between Armenia and Azerbaijan. The problem was not diplomatically resolved, and so, resentment spilled over, and when the people of Nagorno-Karabakh itself voted to join Armenia in 1988, conflict broke out in the region.

For the next six years, fierce fighting continued between the two regions. The collapse of the Soviet Union in 1991, which allowed Armenia and Azerbaijan to gain independence, only briefly slowed down the war. It continued unabated until 1994 when both countries found themselves struggling internally and depleted of resources. Russia stepped in one last time to negotiate a ceasefire that was agreed on May 12th, 1994. At the time, although the war could have gone either way, Armenia undeniably had the upper hand. For the first time in centuries, the little nation was proving itself in warfare.

It was not with violence, however, that Armenia would ultimately solve its problems. As discontent broke out over the series of corrupt presidents and prime ministers that plagued the republic's early years, there were still several instances of violence. The first was on October 27th, 1999, when a group of gunmen entered Parliament and shot the very popular prime minister, who was looking like he was about to turn the country around, dead. The corrupt president, Robert Kocharyan, was conveniently left unhurt. The widespread protests of 2008 that Sargsyan mentioned in his not-so-subtle threat to Pashinyan were another example of Armenia's struggle to find its way out of a history of violence.

Another tragic incident of violence took place in 2015 in what has become known as the Gyumri massacre. It might not have taken hundreds of thousands of lives like the killings that happened a century earlier, but the grisly killing of the entire Avetisyan family—including a toddler and an infant boy—shocked the entire nation. This murder, however, was unlikely to be politically motivated, as the family was just an ordinary, relatively harmless family. The suspect, a teenage Russian soldier with a learning disability, was returned to Russia to stand trial. His motives remain unclear, although conspiracy theories abound.

Three years later, while the latest and most power-hungry in a string of corrupt leaders—Serzh Sargsyan—was in charge of Armenia, Gyumri would once again see history change. But this time, there would be no blood, bullets, or broken glass. There would be no brutal murders. There would be no rapes or gassings or drownings or starving. There would be walking, but this time, it would be done in hope. This time, there would be no Turkish soldiers prodding the weak onward to their deaths. This time, an Armenian man would toss a rucksack on his shoulders and start pacing along the streets, a growing crowd of people following him of their own volition. This time, they would laugh and talk. There would be no screams. There would be no silence. There would be not so much as a thrown stone.

In the Velvet Revolution, the Armenians would take control of their own lives, their own destinies. And they would show the whole of history the power of the Armenian spirit.

Conclusion

In hearing the stories of modern-day Armenians—those who only know the genocide second- or third-hand from the voices of their great-grandparents—a common thread of wariness rings through each tale. This is a people that has suffered enormously, and not just this single generation. Armenians have been suffering ever since the Medes overthrew Urartu nearly three thousand years ago. They have suffered in almost every way conceivable, at the hands of almost any empire you care to name.

Yet, at the same time, there is something robust in their eyes and words. Something fearless, a glimmer of that tenacity that had Hayk draw back his bow on the shores of Lake Van, a spark of the vision that drove Tigranes the Great to build the Armenian Empire. There is a willingness there to buckle down and work hard. This is a people that are afraid to trust, a people that have seen too much and suffered far too many evils. But this is also a people ready for a new beginning. A people who feel responsible for their own fate.

What has changed since the days that a disheartened Armenia allowed itself to be tossed back and forth between Rome and Parthia, the Byzantines and the Sasanids, Turkey and Russia? The change was forged on the flanks of the mountains surrounding Sardarapat, where a group of Armenian volunteers grabbed whatever weapons they could find and made a final stand against the oncoming Ottomans. In the face of genocide, the very destruction of their people, Armenians stood together to cry no more. They put the Ottomans to flight, and they realized that they alone were responsible for their own people.

So, when Serzh Sargsyan told Nikol Pashinyan that the responsibility was his own, Pashinyan was as ready for it as Drastamat Kanayan had been at Sardarapat. At Sardarapat, the Armenians underwent a messy rebirth in blood and agony. But starting in Gyumri and undertaking the long walk to Yerevan, this people have proven something even more powerful. They have proven that a nation can heal from even the most devastating crime of all, genocide.

It remains to be seen whether Pashinyan's government really will bring about the hope that Armenians have for the future. Yet even if it does not, one gets the feeling looking into the eyes of the Armenians that this people will survive. In fact, they will do more than survive. Surviving was what they did during the genocide. Today, with a revolution of peace, with a spirit of hope and courage, they will do so much more than that. They will thrive.

And they might just show the rest of the world how to do that, against all the odds.

Here's another book you might be interested in

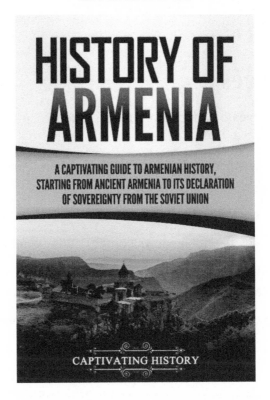

Sources

http://100years100facts.com/facts/garden-eden-traditions-located-armenia/

https://www.peopleofar.com/2013/12/02/armenia-the-forgotten-paradise/

https://bible.knowing-jesus.com/Genesis/2/type/kjv

https://www.thevintagenews.com/2019/05/08/areni-1/

https://www.thevintagenews.com/2017/06/02/the-areni-1-shoe-the-oldest-leather-shoe-in-the-world-was-found-in-a-cave-in-armenia/

https://www.atlasobscura.com/places/areni-1-cave-complex

https://www.ancient.eu/Areni_Cave/

https://www.ancient.eu/Tushpa/

https://www.livius.org/articles/place/tuspa-van/

https://www.christianity.com/church/denominations/discover-the-assyrians-10-things-to-know-about-their-history-faith.html

https://books.google.co.za/books?id=OR_PHoKZ6ycC&pg=PA67&lpg=PA67&dq=aramu+urartu&source=bl&ots=e_ZxonHPrQ&sig=ACfU3U36PTCJ0iihLc2ZZ8sNKG10USso3A&hl=en&sa=X&ved=2ahUKEwi5qMfC_-

bkAhVFXRUIHfbXDikQ6AEwEXoECAwQAQ#v=onepage&q=ara
mu%20urartu&f=false

https://tamarnajarian.wordpress.com/2012/02/17/arame-king-of-urartu/

https://www.ancient.eu/Urartu_Civilization/

https://www.degruyter.com/view/j/jah.2016.4.issue-1/jah-2015-0024/jah-2015-0024.xml

http://bronze-age-towns.over-blog.com/2016/12/musri-or-musasir-the-city-of-mudjesir.html

https://www.britannica.com/place/Urartu

https://www.livius.org/articles/people/medes/

https://www.britannica.com/place/Media-ancient-region-Iran

https://www.ancient.eu/Cyrus_the_Great/

https://www.nationalgeographic.com/culture/people/reference/cyrus-the-great/

https://www.history.com/topics/religion/zoroastrianism

https://www.youtube.com/watch?v=lP5RqosiYQA

https://www.ancient-origins.net/history-famous-people/mithridates-vi-pontus-poison-king-pontus-and-aggravation-rome-005907

https://www.thoughtco.com/pompey-the-great-pompeius-magnus-112662

https://www.livius.org/articles/person/tigranes-ii/

https://www.ancient.eu/Tigranes_the_Great/

https://www.britannica.com/biography/Lucius-Licinius-Lucullus

https://www.britannica.com/biography/Tigranes-II-the-Great

https://www.ancient-origins.net/history/rise-and-fall-tigranes-great-king-armenia-002815

https://www.ancient.eu/pompey/

https://www.britannica.com/biography/Vonones-I

https://www.britannica.com/biography/Artavasdes-II

https://www.historynet.com/mark-antonys-persian-campaign.htm

https://www.encyclopedia.com/religion/encyclopedias-almanacs-transcripts-and-maps/tiridates-iii-armenian-king

https://www.ancient-origins.net/history-famous-people/diocletian-0010984?utm_source=feedburner&utm_medium=feed&utm_campaign=Feed%3A+AncientOrigins+%28Ancient+Origins%29

https://www.christianity.com/church/church-history/timeline/1-300/yield-or-suffer-said-diocletian-11629633.html

https://allinnet.info/news/the-goddess-of-love-and-fertility-anahit-ancient-armenia-preface/

https://www.ancient.eu/article/801/the-early-christianization-of-armenia/

http://www.iranchamber.com/history/parthians/parthians.php

http://factsanddetails.com/central-asia/Central_Asian_Topics/sub8_8a/entry-4502.html#chapter-10

https://www.livius.org/articles/person/vologases-iv/

https://www.historynet.com/romes-parthian-war-d-161-166.htm

https://www.ancient.eu/armenia/

https://www.britannica.com/biography/Saint-Mesrop-Mashtots

https://www.thevintagenews.com/2017/01/31/mesrop-mashtots-plight-for-the-armenian-alphabet-and-language/

https://www.britannica.com/topic/Armenian-language

https://armeniadiscovery.com/en/articles/mesrop-mashtots-the-creator-of-the-armenian-alphabet

https://www.deseret.com/2018/3/16/20641780/armenia-the-first-christian-nation

https://www.ancient.eu/Arsacid_Dynasty_of_Armenia/

https://www.ancient.eu/article/801/the-early-christianization-of-armenia/

https://www.thoughtco.com/war-elephants-in-asian-history-195817

https://www.ancient-origins.net/history/war-elephants-military-tanks-ancient-world-009967

https://www.ancient-origins.net/history/immortals-elite-army-persian-empire-never-grew-weak-002321

https://www.ancient.eu/image/8231/battle-of-avarayr/

https://armenianchurch.us/essential_grid/st-vartan-and-the-battle-of-avarayr/

https://www.britannica.com/biography/Saint-Vardan-Mamikonian#ref1078407

https://www.livius.org/articles/person/heraclius/

https://www.ancient-origins.net/history-famous-people/heraclius-0011027

https://www.ancient.eu/article/1207/byzantine-armenian-relations/

https://www.britannica.com/biography/Maurice-Byzantine-emperor

https://www.encyclopedia.com/religion/encyclopedias-almanacs-transcripts-and-maps/maurice-byzantine-emperor

https://www.livius.org/articles/person/phocas/

https://www.britannica.com/biography/Phocas

http://www.fsmitha.com/h3/islam04.htm

https://www.ancient.eu/Dvin/

https://www.history.com/topics/religion/islam

http://www.armenian-history.com/Nyuter/HISTORY/middle%20ages/Armenia_%20in_7th_and_%208th_centuries.htm

https://www.peopleofar.com/2019/01/05/the-forgotten-kingdom-bagratid-armenia/

https://www.peopleofar.com/2014/01/13/ani-city-of-1001-churches-2/

https://www.peopleofar.com/2012/01/28/armenian-crusaders/

https://www.medievalists.net/2011/07/the-crusaders-through-armenian-eyes/

https://www.thoughtco.com/who-were-the-seljuks-195399

https://www.ancient.eu/First_Crusade/

http://historyofarmenia.org/2017/04/23/mongols-invade-armenia/

https://www.britannica.com/biography/Levon-I

https://allinnet.info/history/levon-the-great-king-of-cilicia-the-armenian-rubenid-dynasty/

https://www.panorama.am/en/news/2016/03/07/Aris-Ghazinyan/1539066

https://www.bbc.com/news/magazine-20538810

https://www.thoughtco.com/timur-or-tamerlane-195675

https://www.britannica.com/biography/Timur

https://www.britannica.com/place/Little-Armenia

https://www.thoughtco.com/who-were-the-mamluks-195371

https://www.nationalgeographic.com/culture/people/reference/mongols/

https://www.thoughtco.com/genghis-khan-195669

https://www.theguardian.com/world/2015/apr/24/armenian-genocide-survivors-stories-my-dreams-cannot-mourn

https://www.armenian-genocide.org/adana.html

https://www.britannica.com/topic/Hamidian-massacres

https://www.history.com/topics/world-war-i/armenian-genocide

http://www.armeniapedia.org/wiki/Armenian_Soviet_Socialist_Repu
blic

https://mirrorspectator.com/2018/05/24/the-battle-of-sardarapat-and-
its-aftermath/

http://historyofarmenia.org/2017/05/28/battle-sardarabad-birth-new-
nation/

http://www.panarmenian.net/eng/details/179324/

https://www.youtube.com/watch?v=cQanB0lR81A

https://www.azatutyun.am/a/26806241.html

https://www.rferl.org/a/armenians-speak-one-year-on-from-
revolution/29898637.html

https://www.tandfonline.com/doi/abs/10.1080/10999922.2019.15810
42?af=R&journalCode=mpin20

https://griffithreview.atavist.com/life-after-genocide

Illustration I: By www.armenica.orgUploaded to en.wikipedia by
en:user:Nareklm - Armenica.orgUploaded to en.wikipedia:
en:Image:20tigranes95-66.gifThe original source of the Map is:
Robert H. Hewsen "Armenia: A Historical Atlas". The University of
Chicago Press, 2001 ISBN 978-0-226-33228-4. Map 20 (The Empire
of Tigran the Great, 95-66 BC), page 34., CC BY-SA 3.0,
https://commons.wikimedia.org/w/index.php?curid=1557220

Illustration   II:
https://commons.wikimedia.org/wiki/File:The_battle_of_Avarayr.jp
g

Illustration   III:
https://commons.wikimedia.org/wiki/File:Church_ruins_in_Ani.jpg

---

Illustration IV: By Unknown - File:Ravished Armenia.djvu p. 10, Public Domain, https://commons.wikimedia.org/w/index.php?curid=18092075

Illustration V: By MEDIACRAT, CC BY-SA 3.0, https://commons.wikimedia.org/w/index.php?curid=11600921

Made in the USA
Monee, IL
14 January 2021

57613432R00069